Serenity Mandalas

A Mindful Coloring Journey for Adults

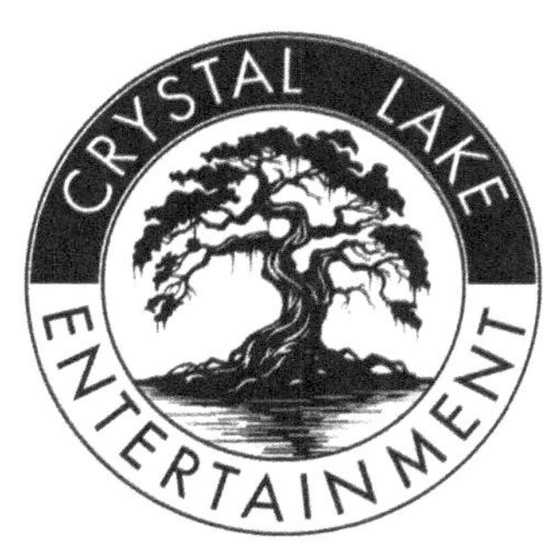

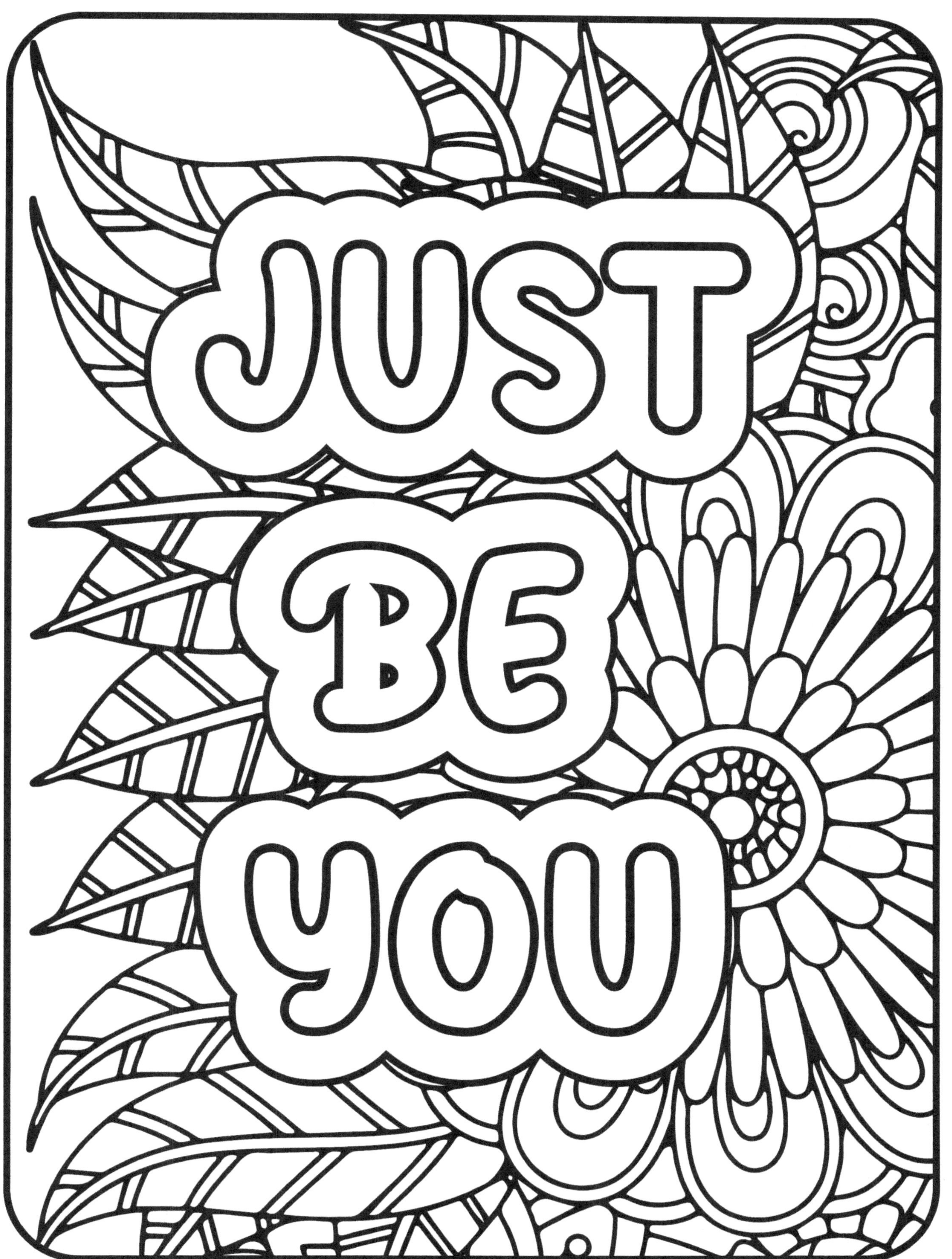

JUST
BE
YOU

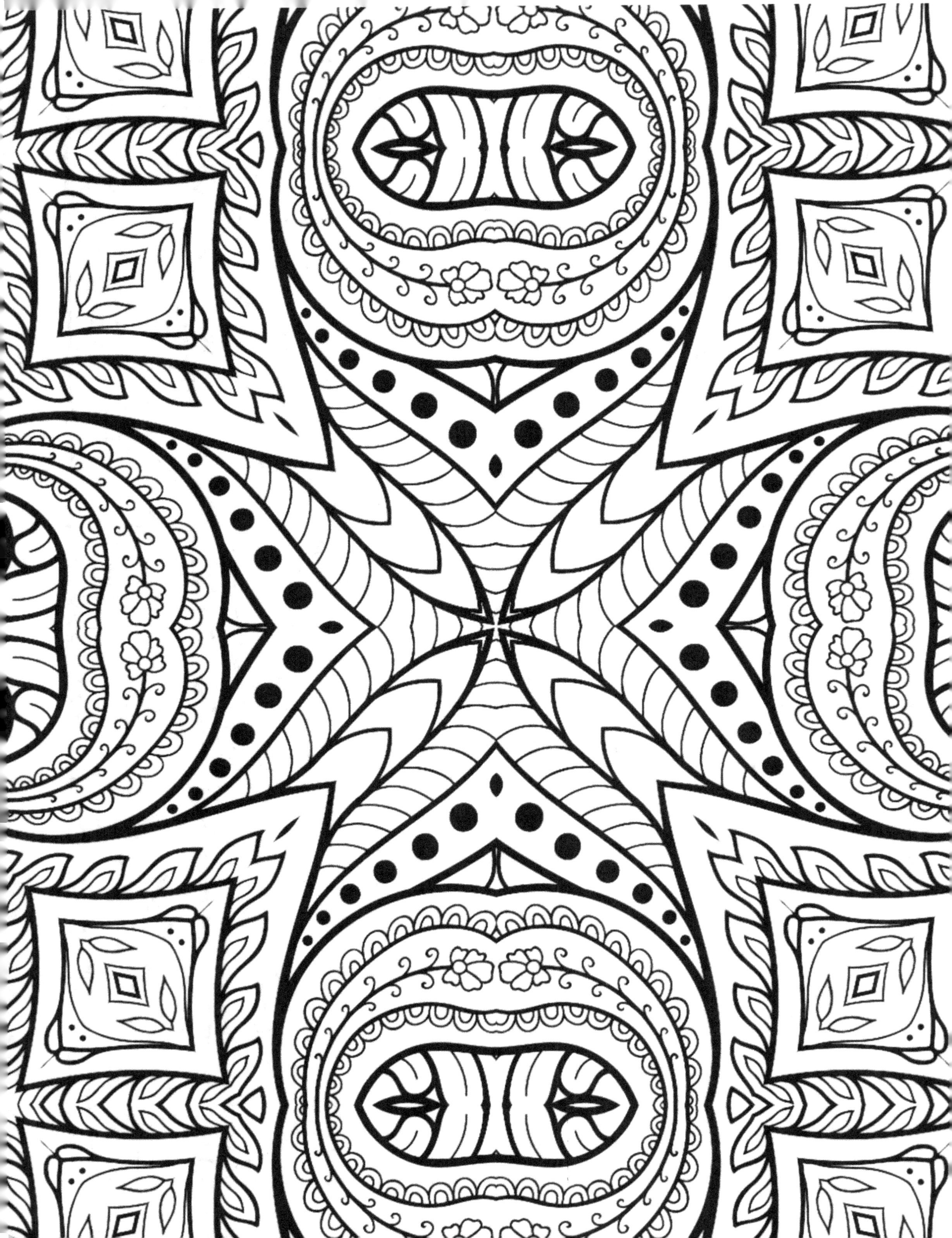

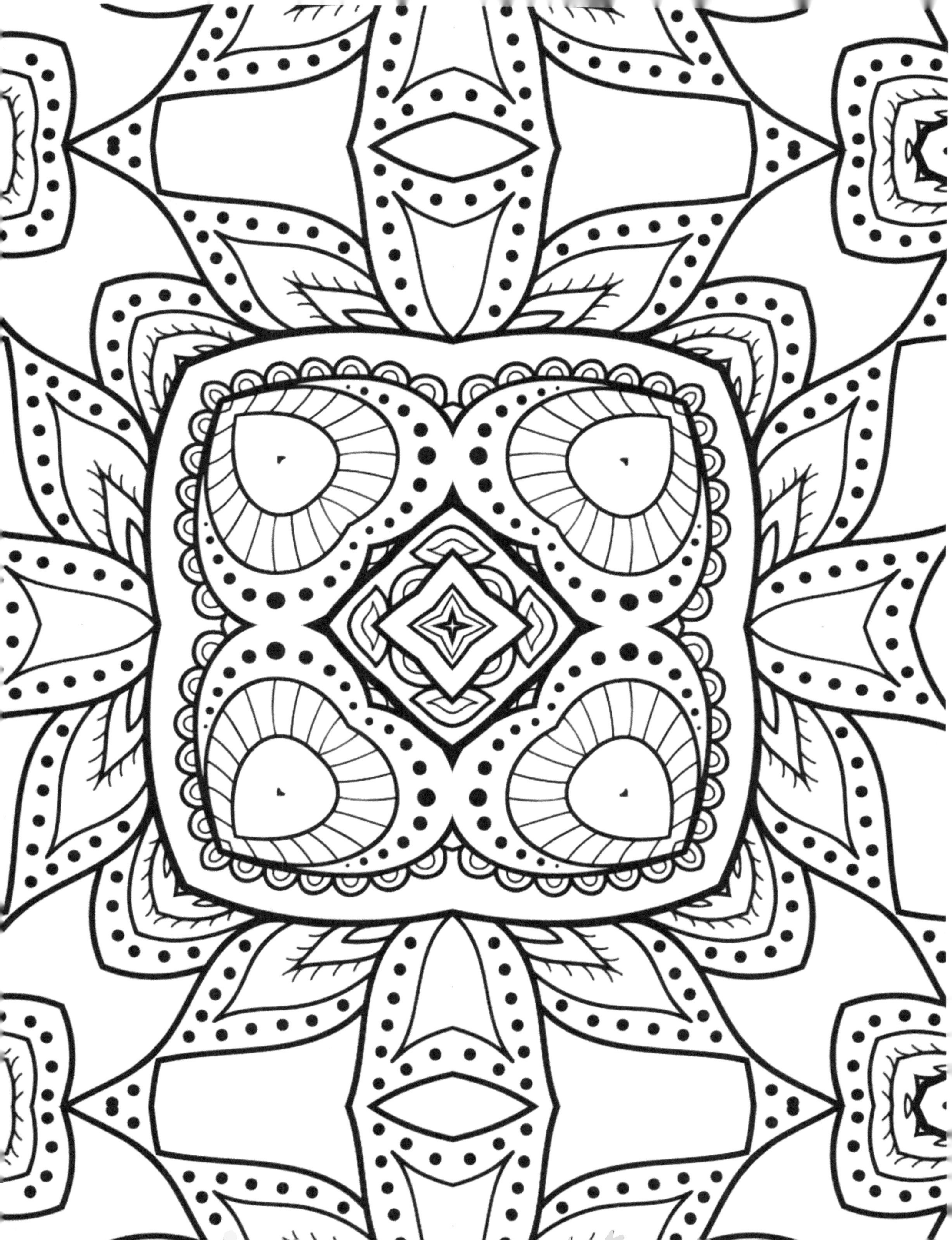

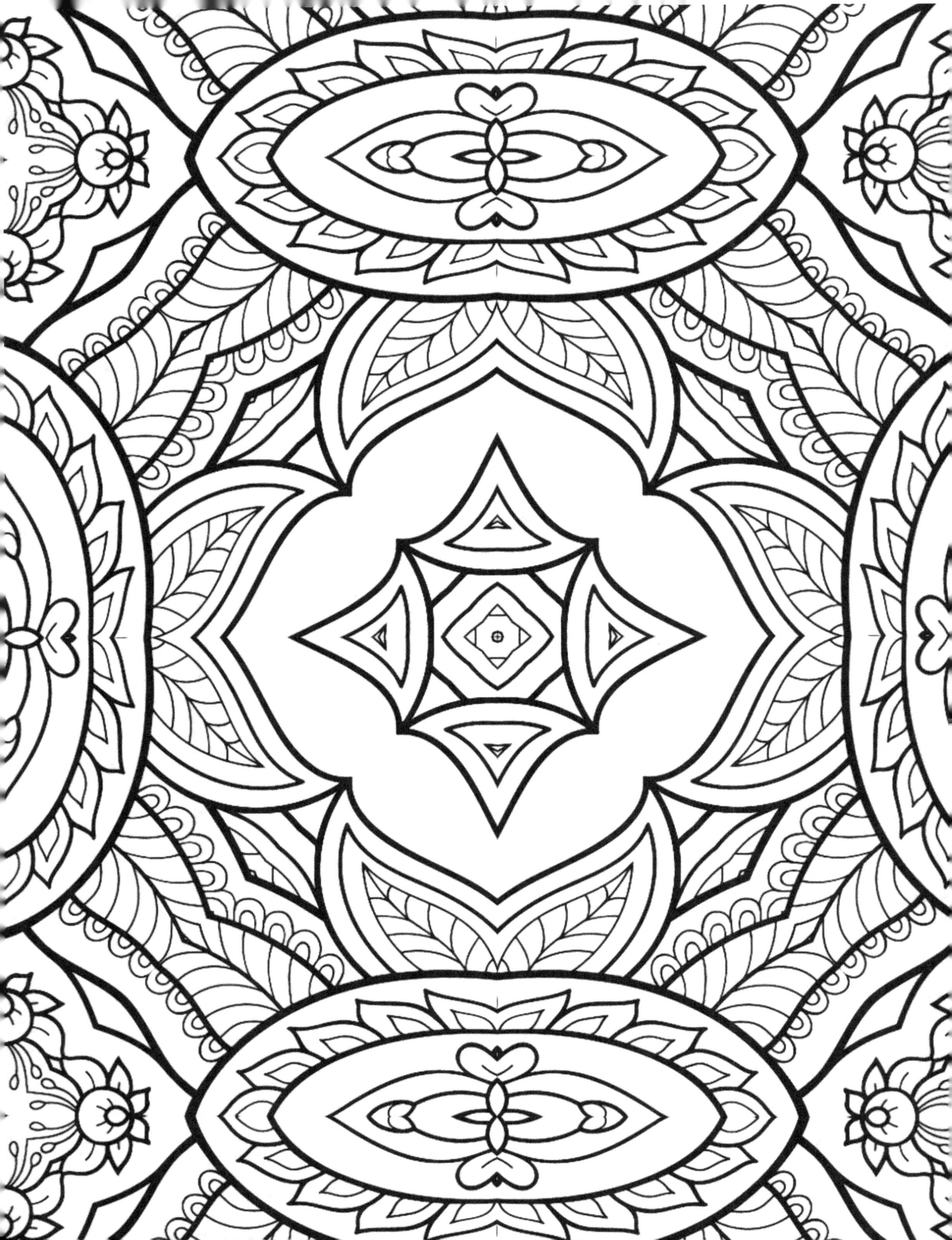

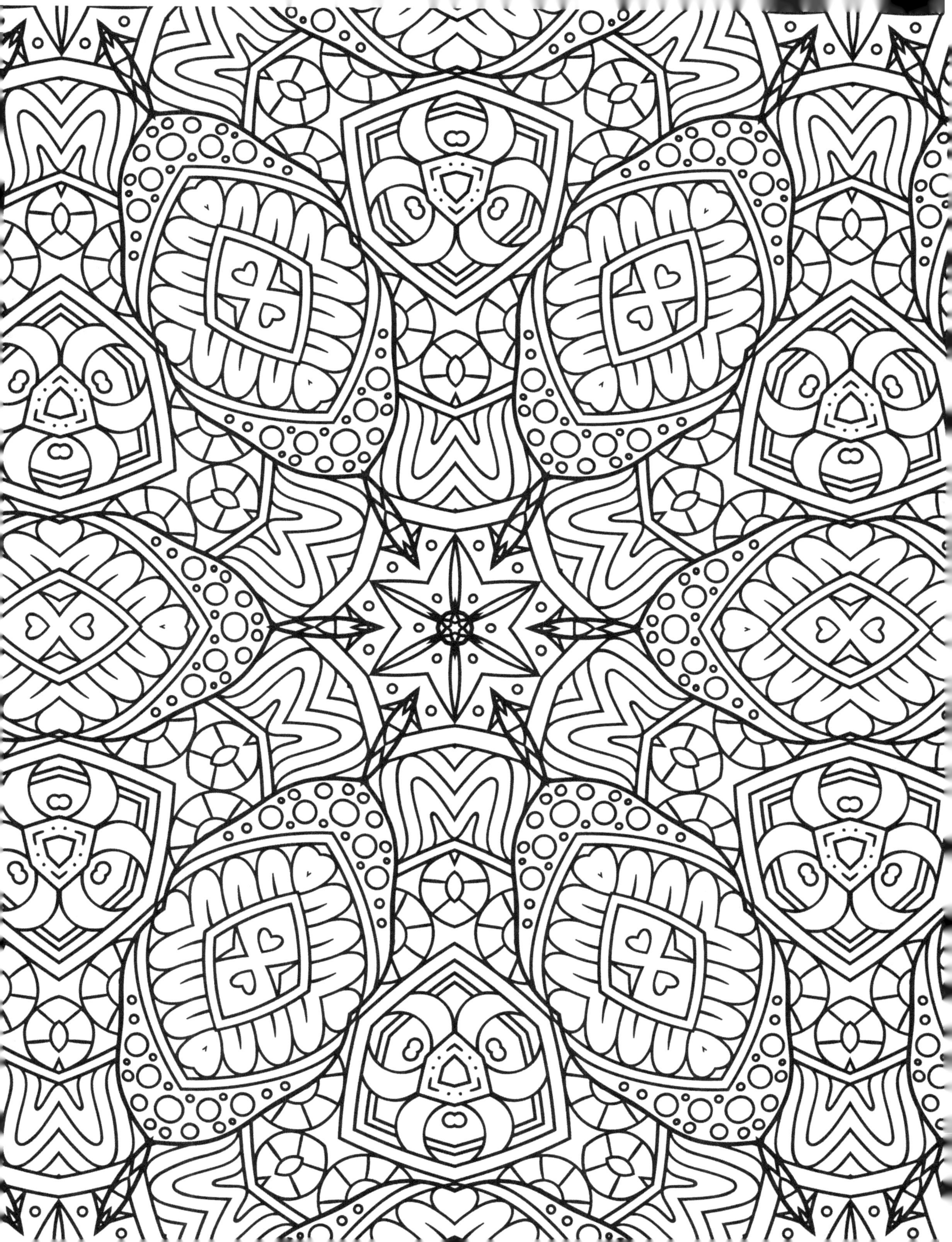

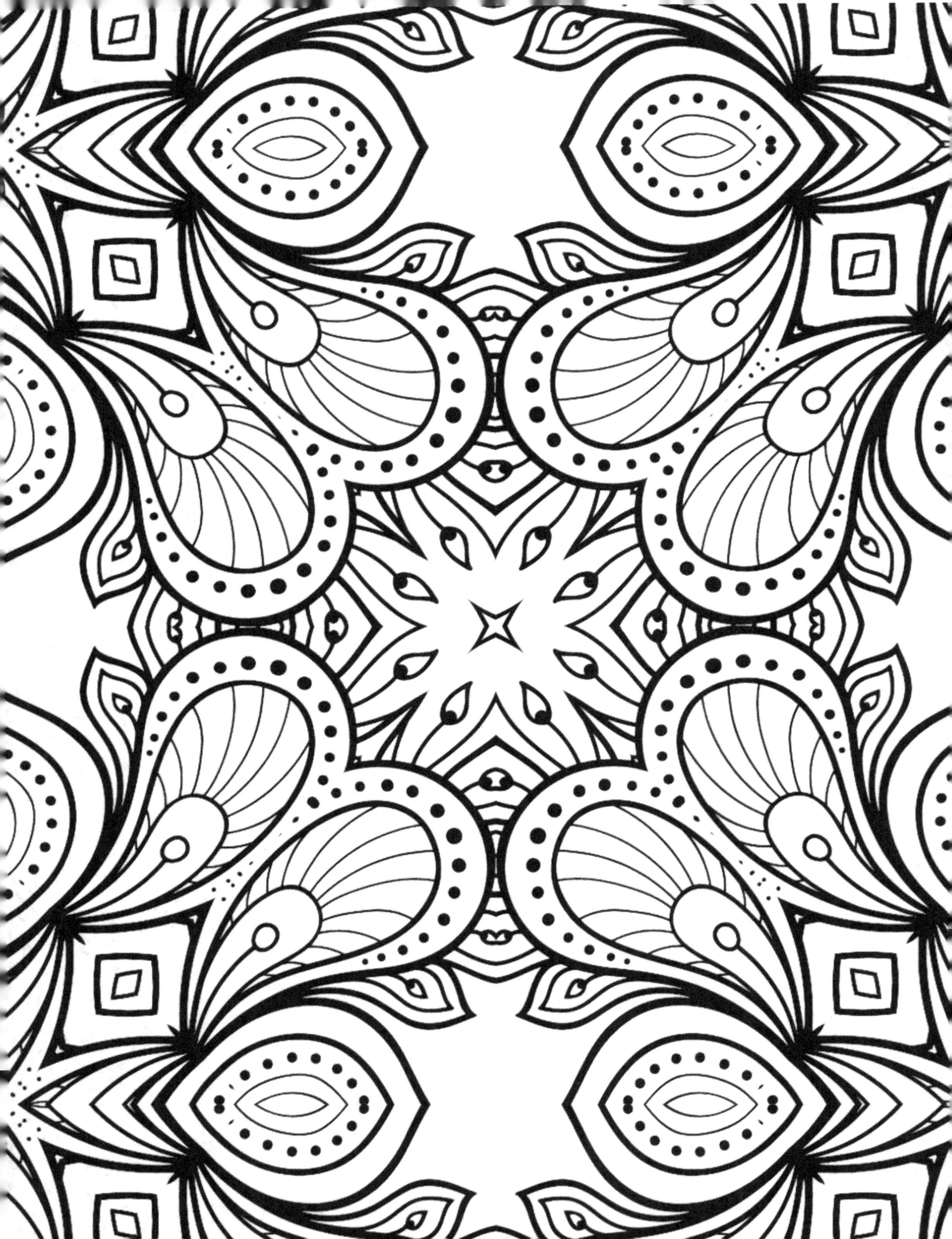

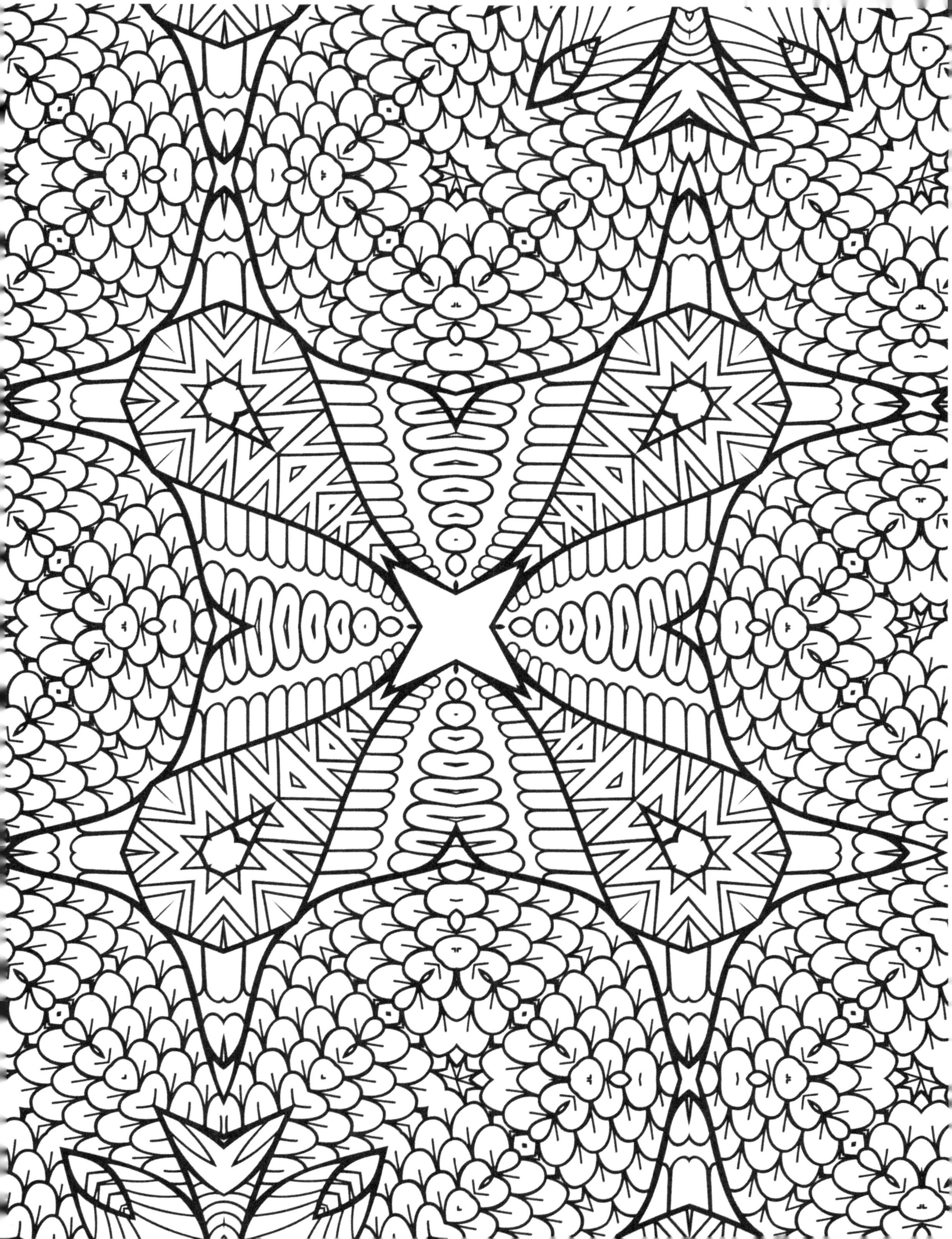

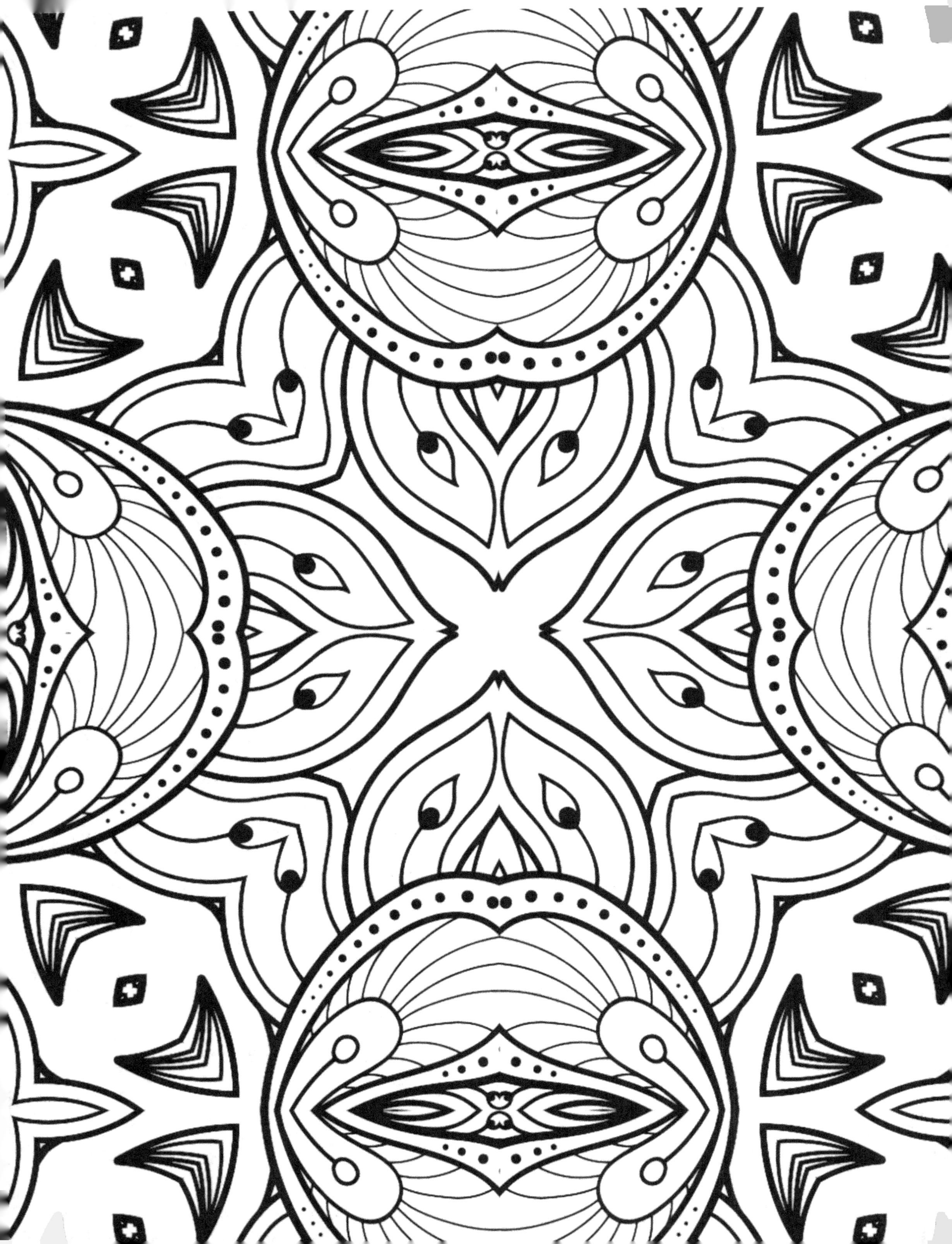

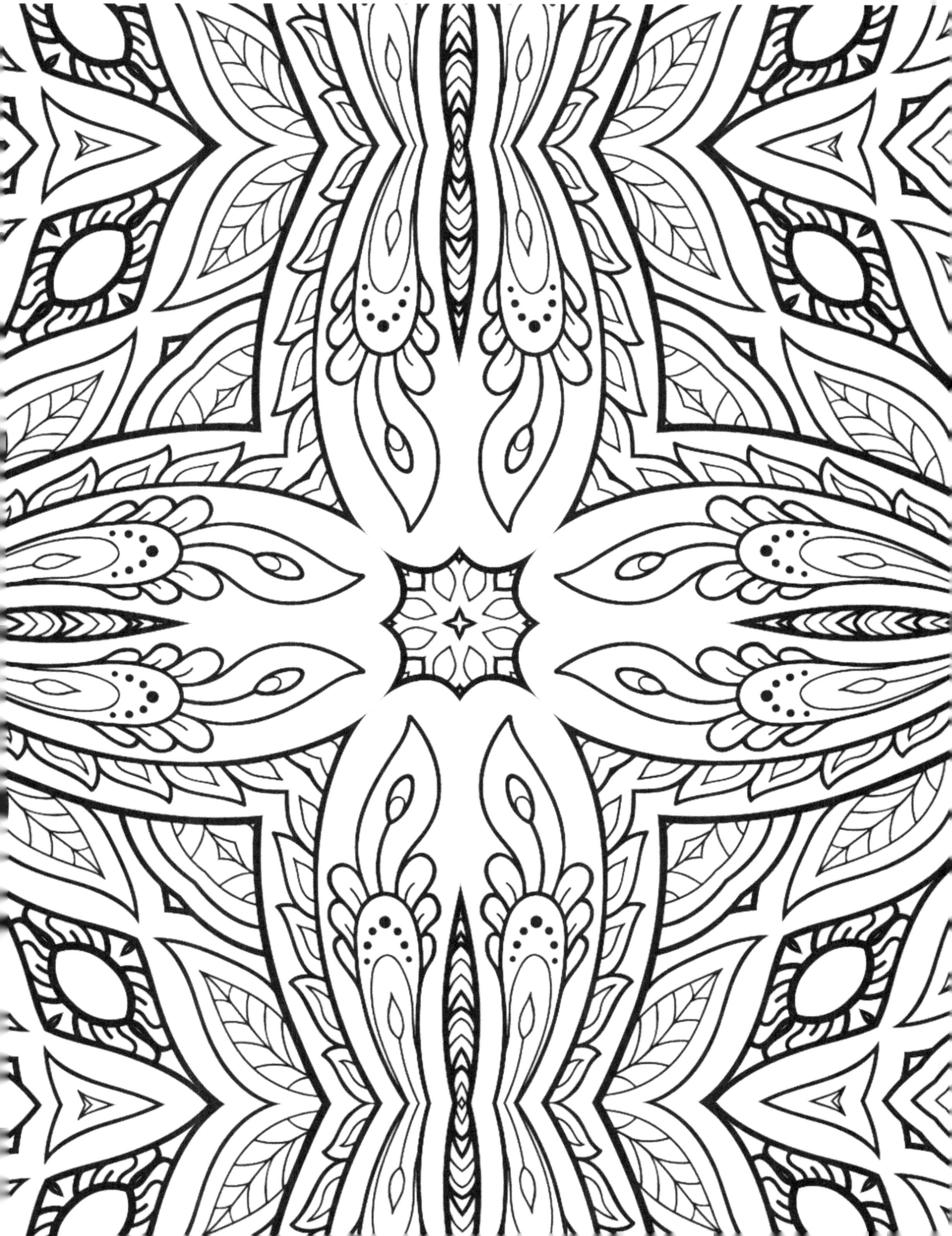

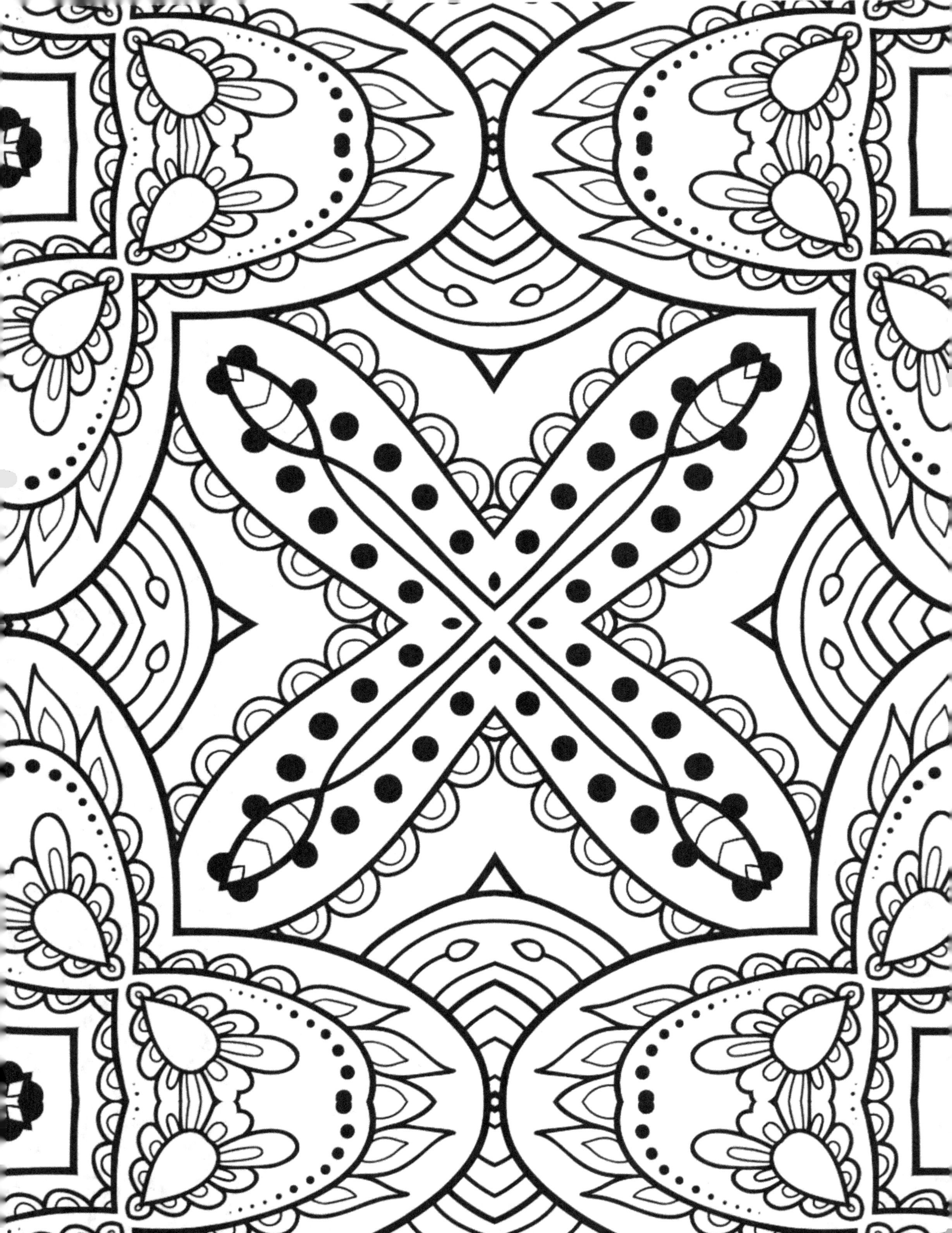

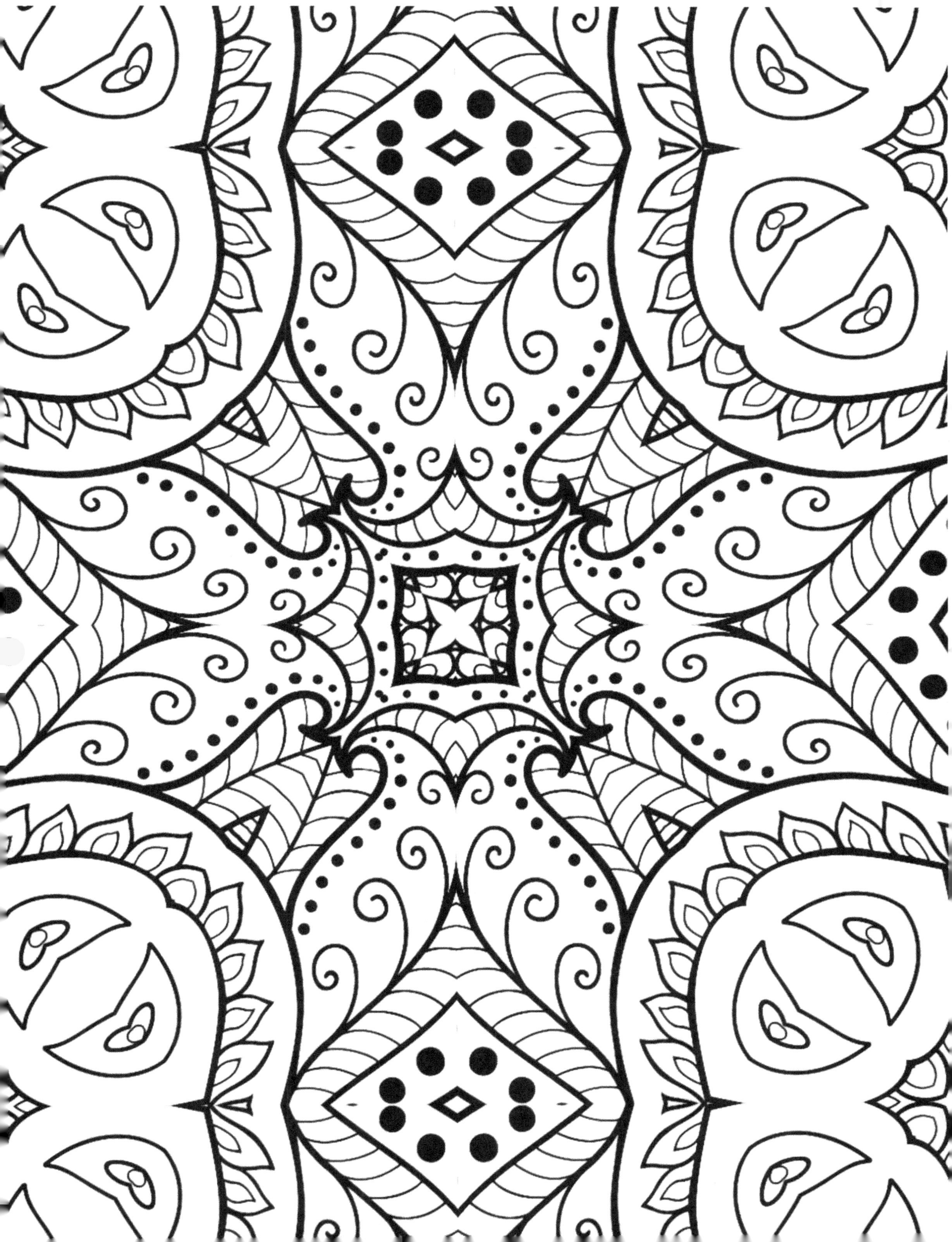

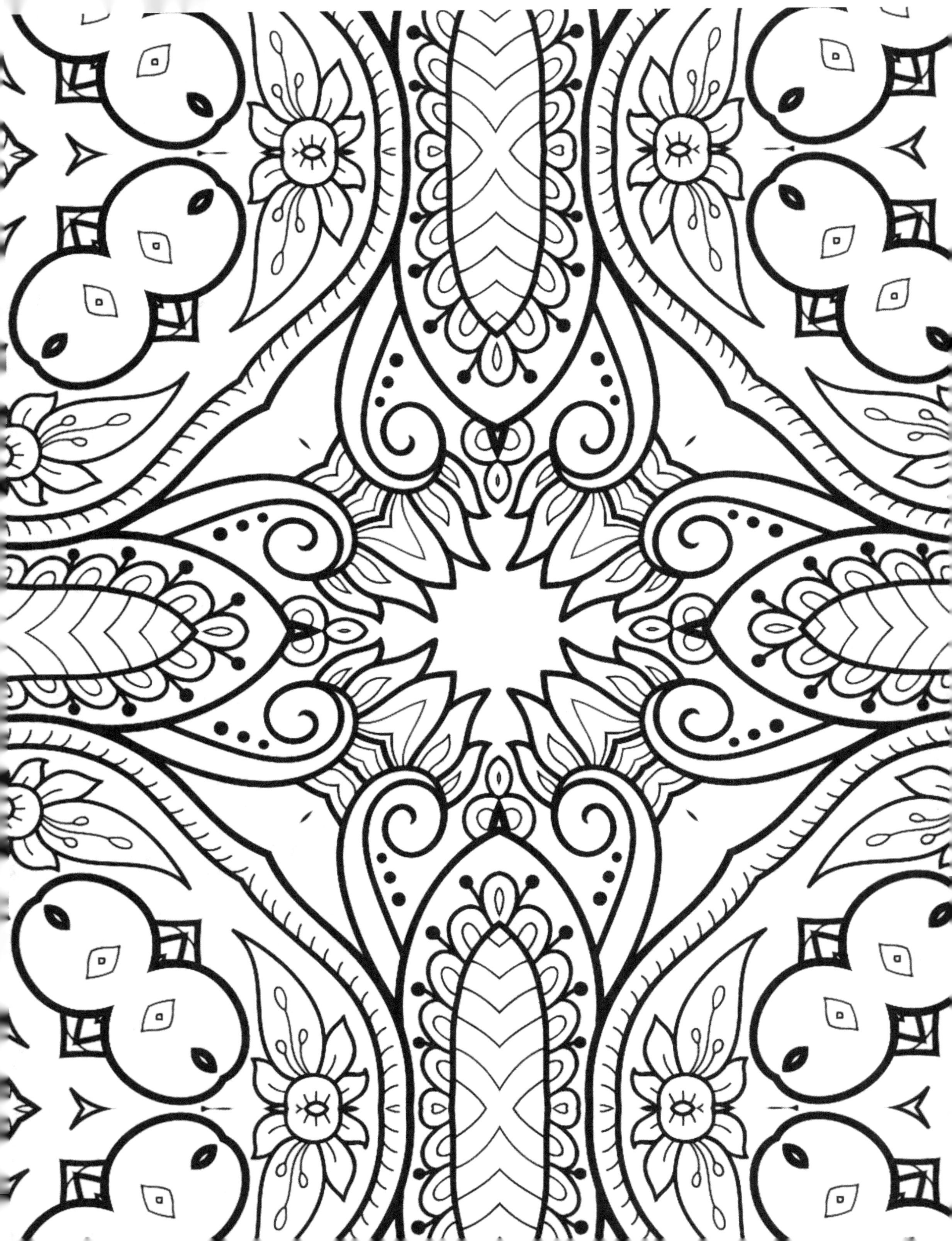

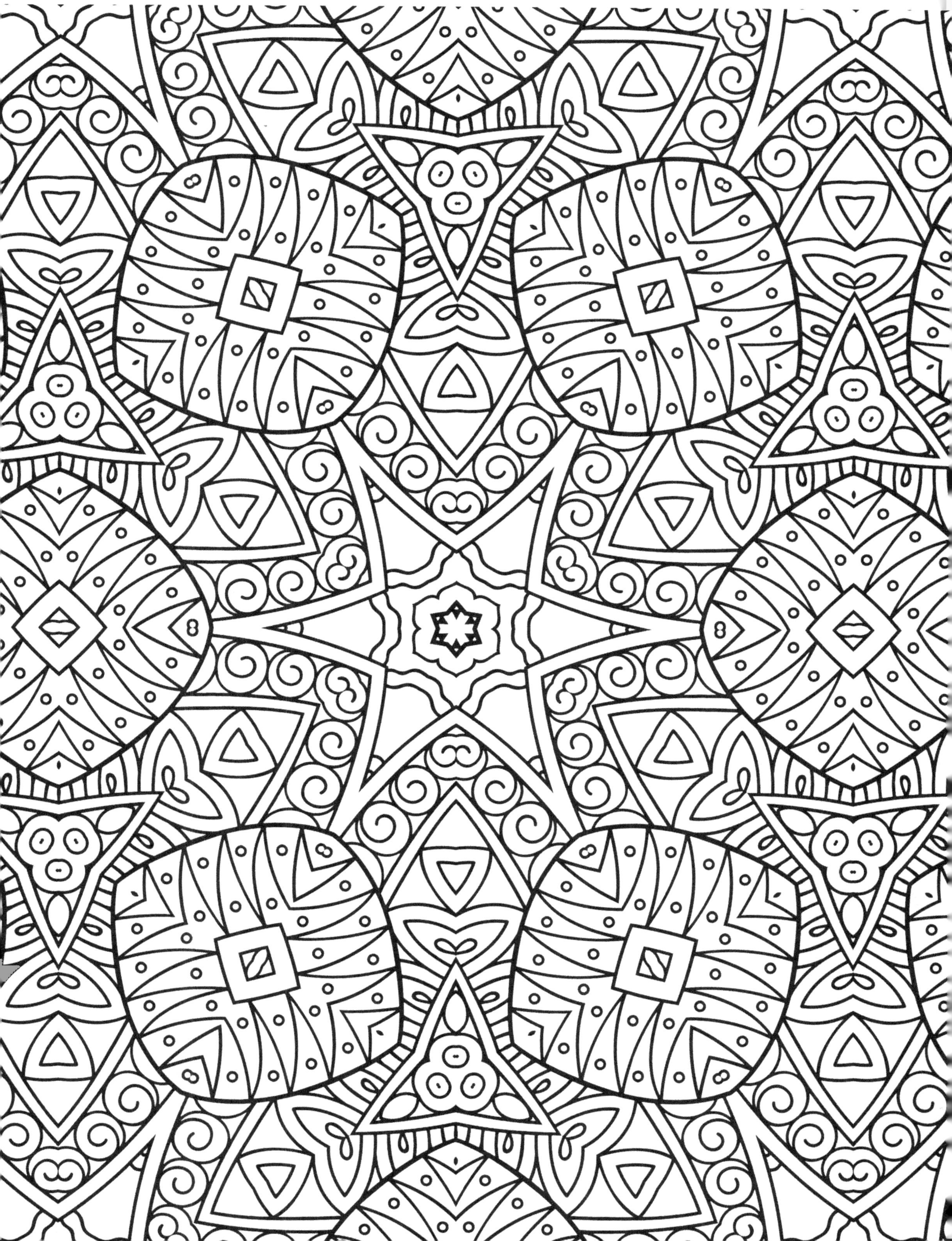

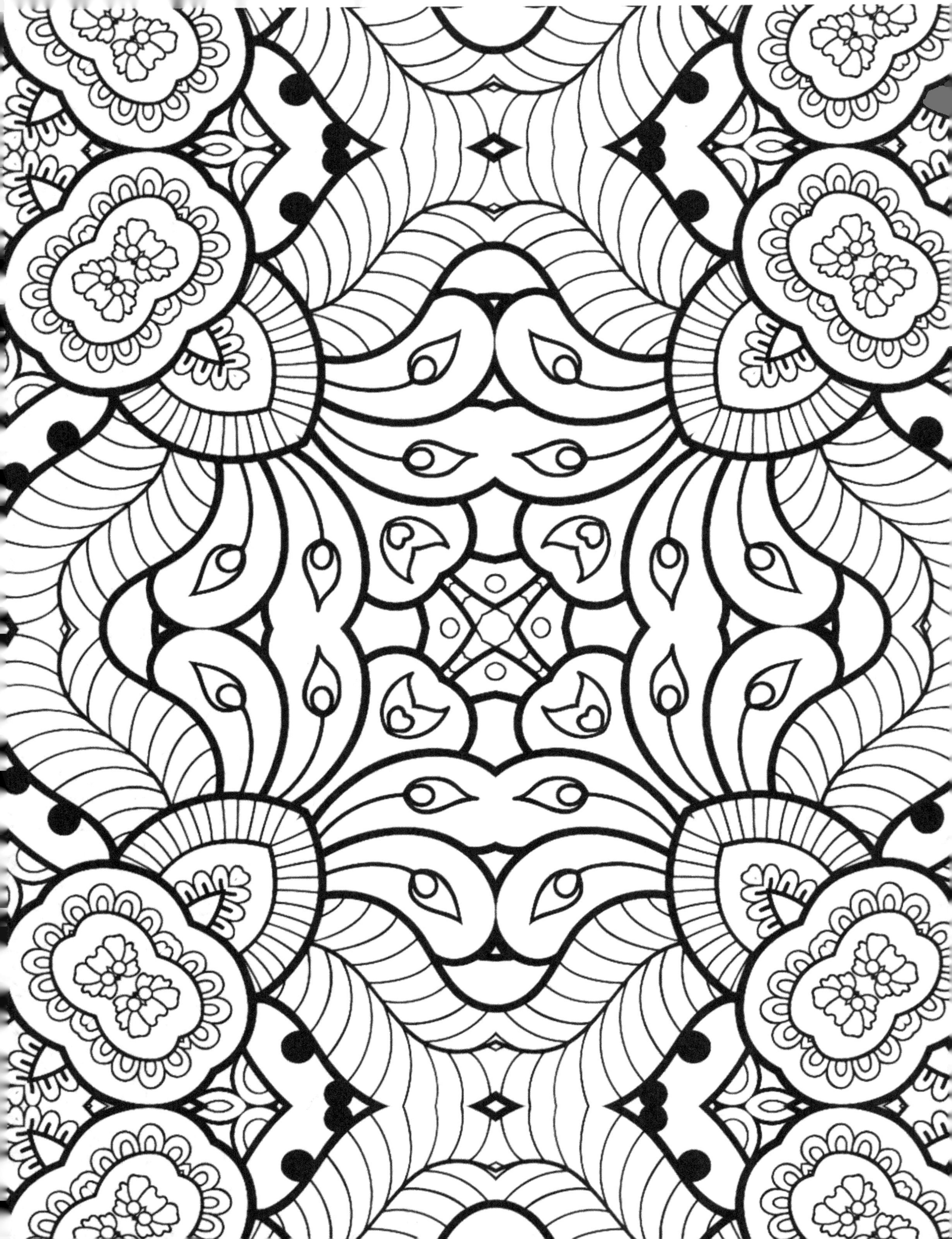

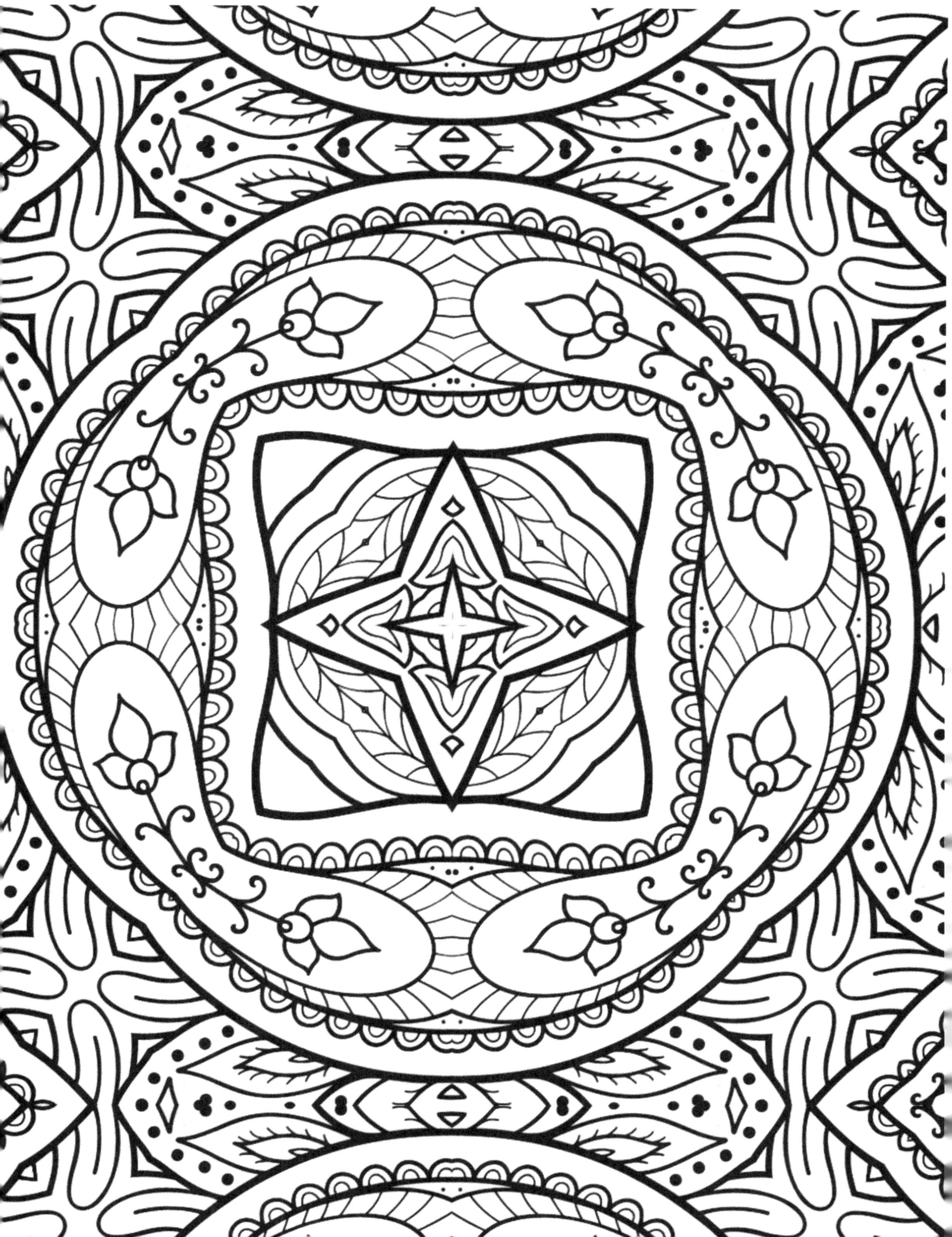

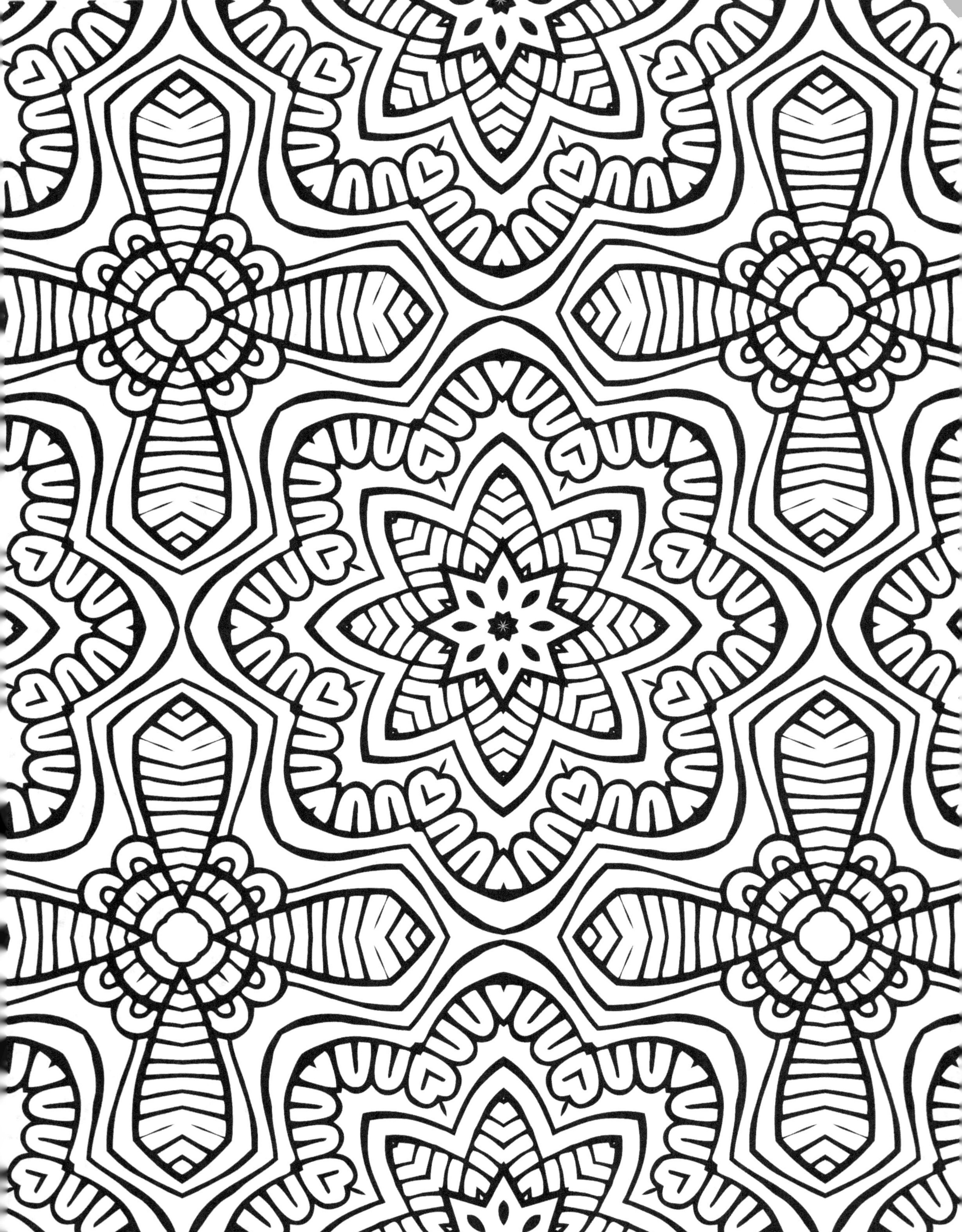

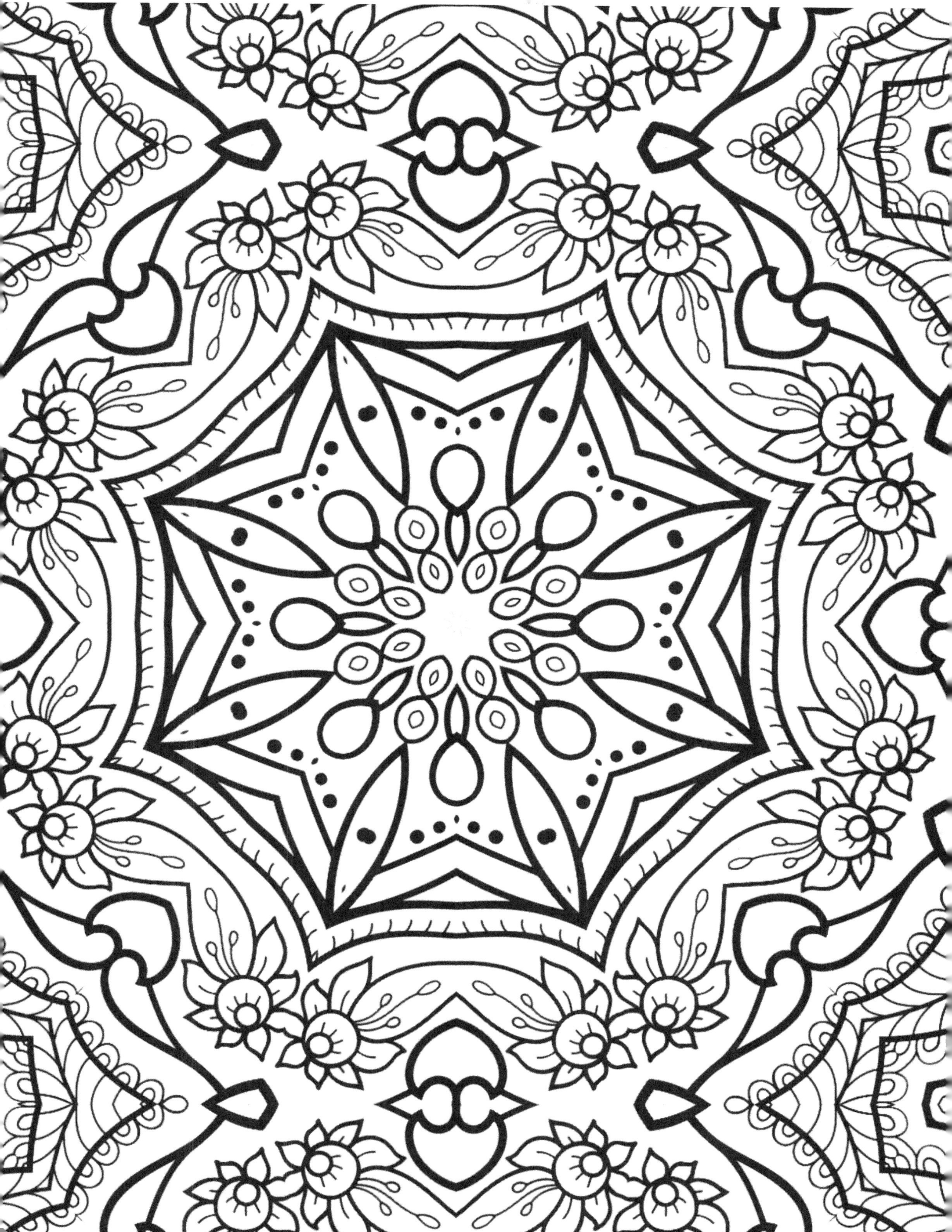

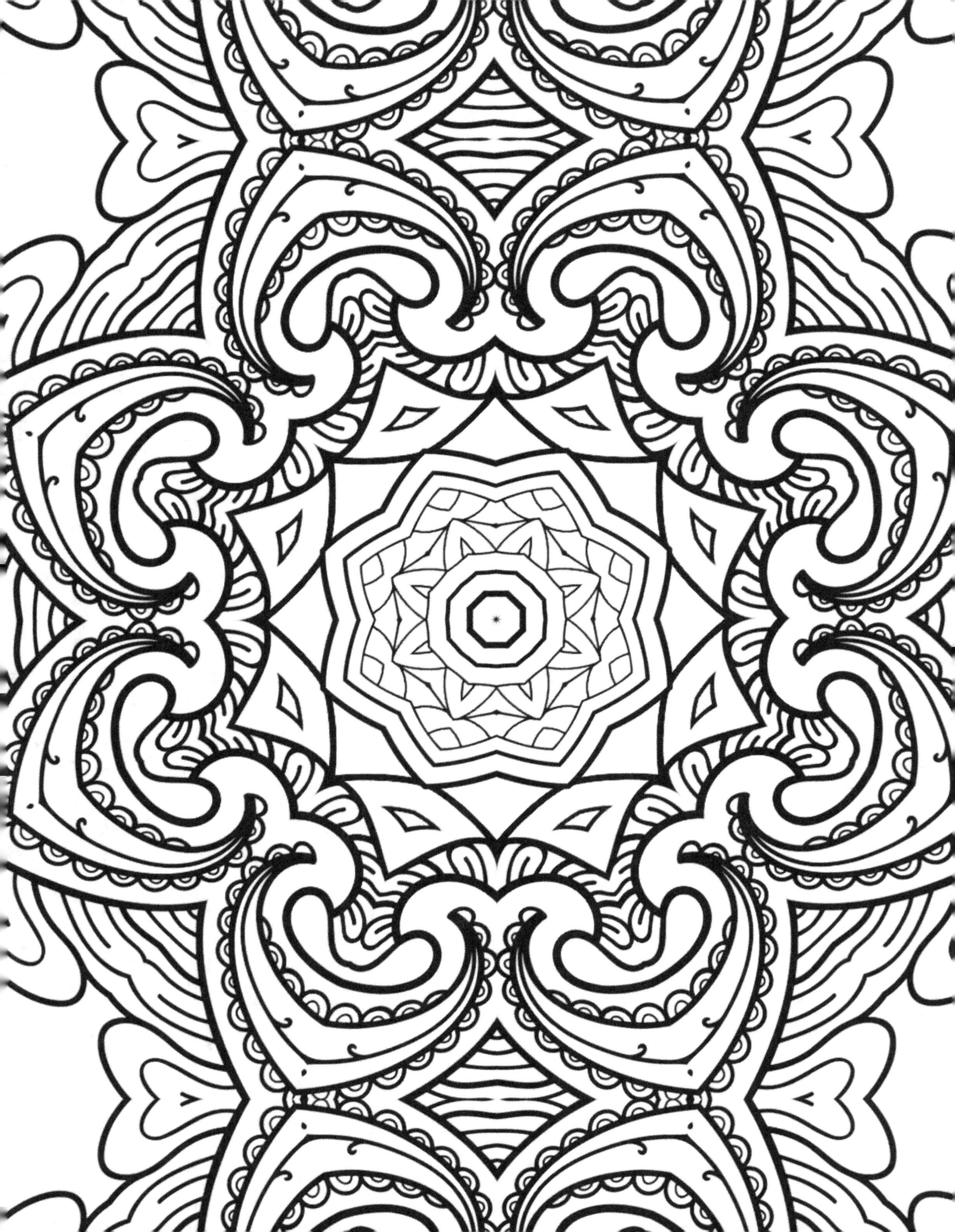

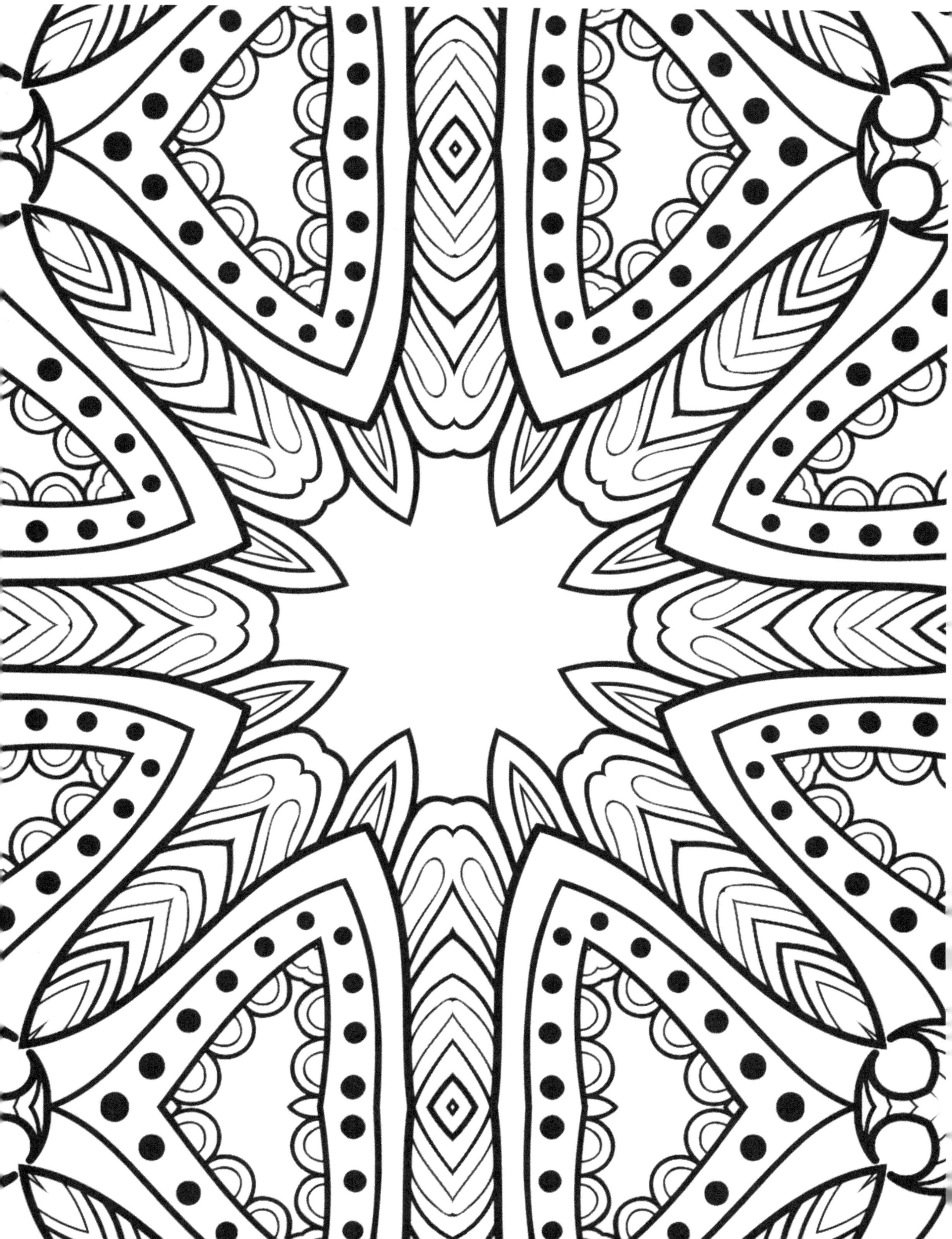

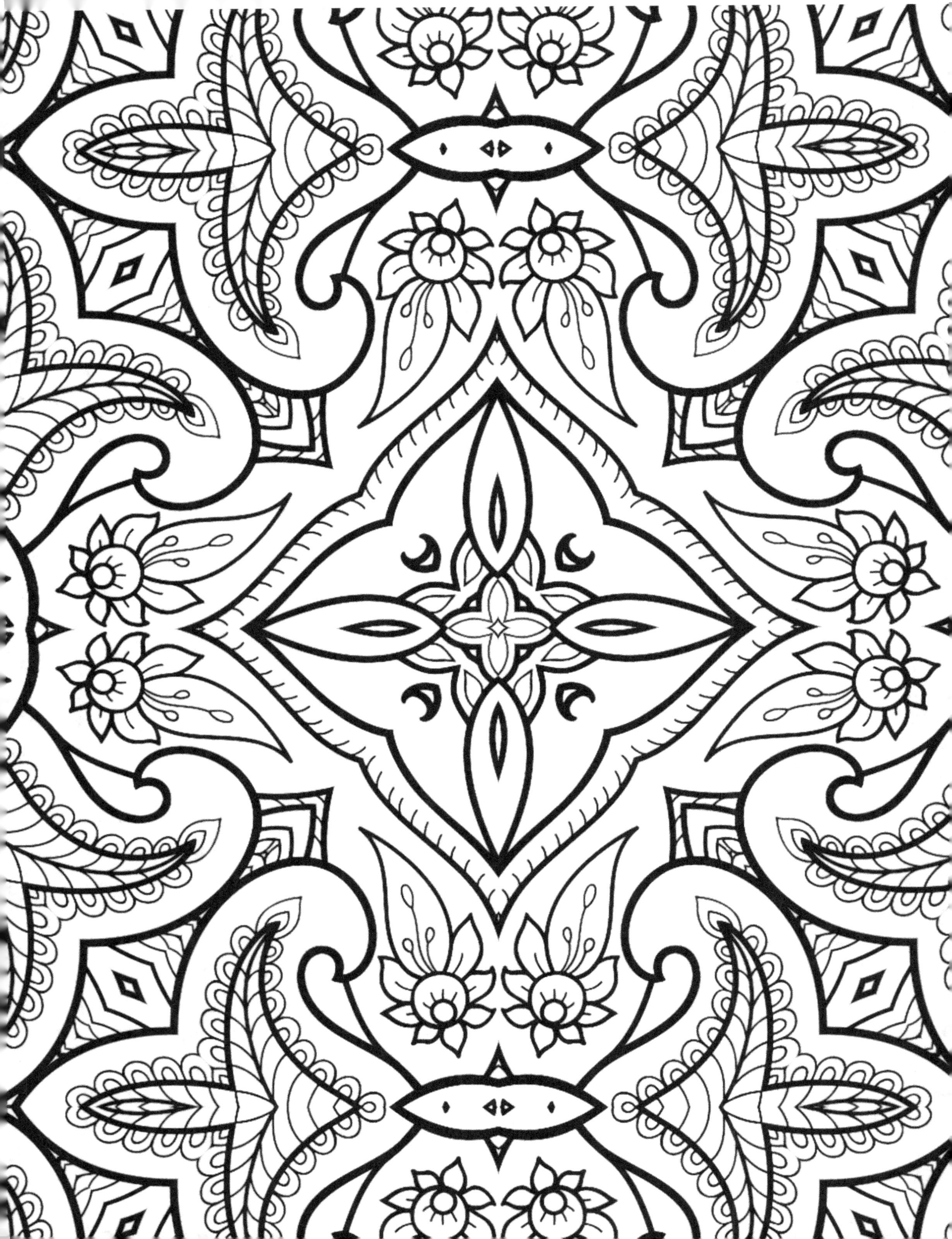

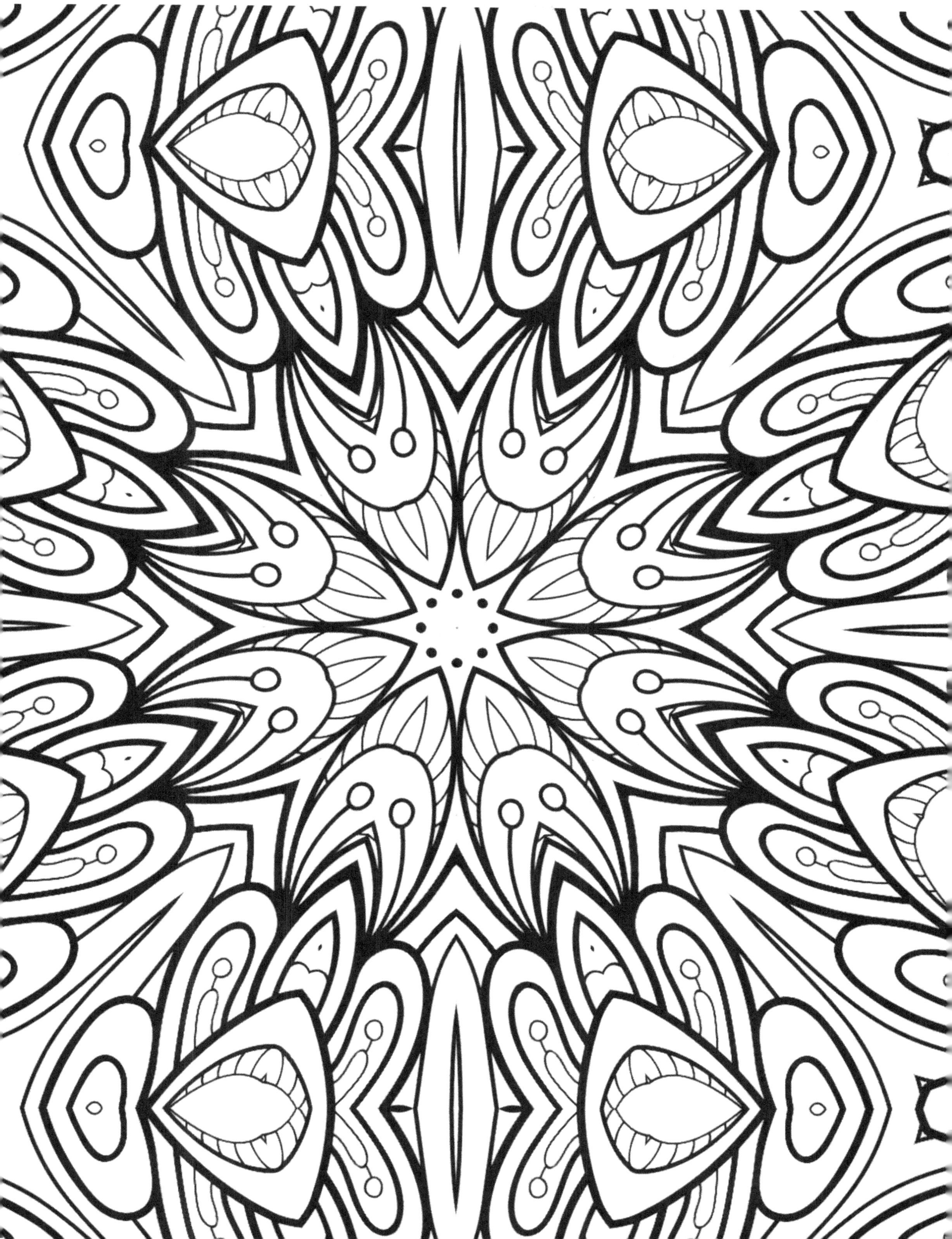

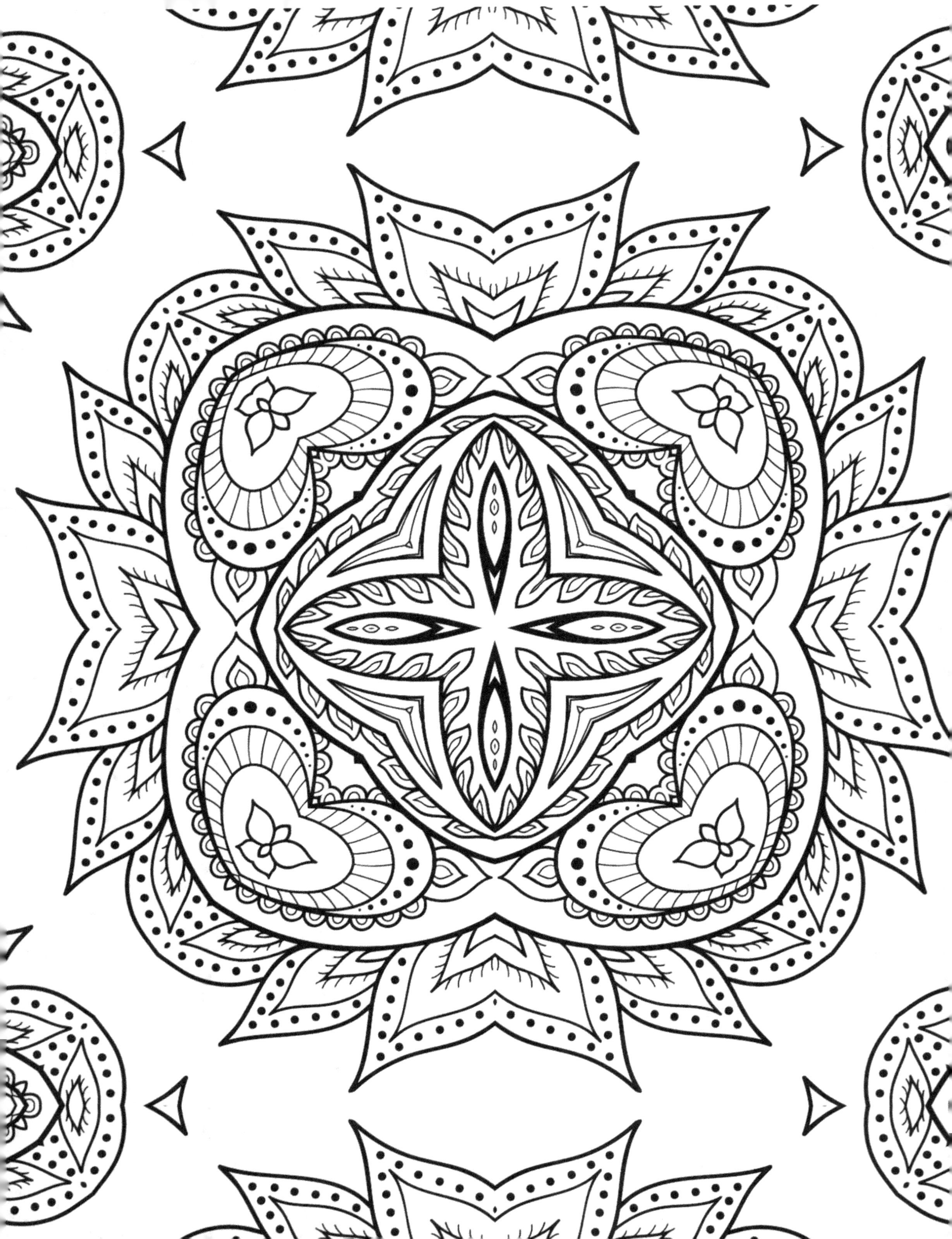

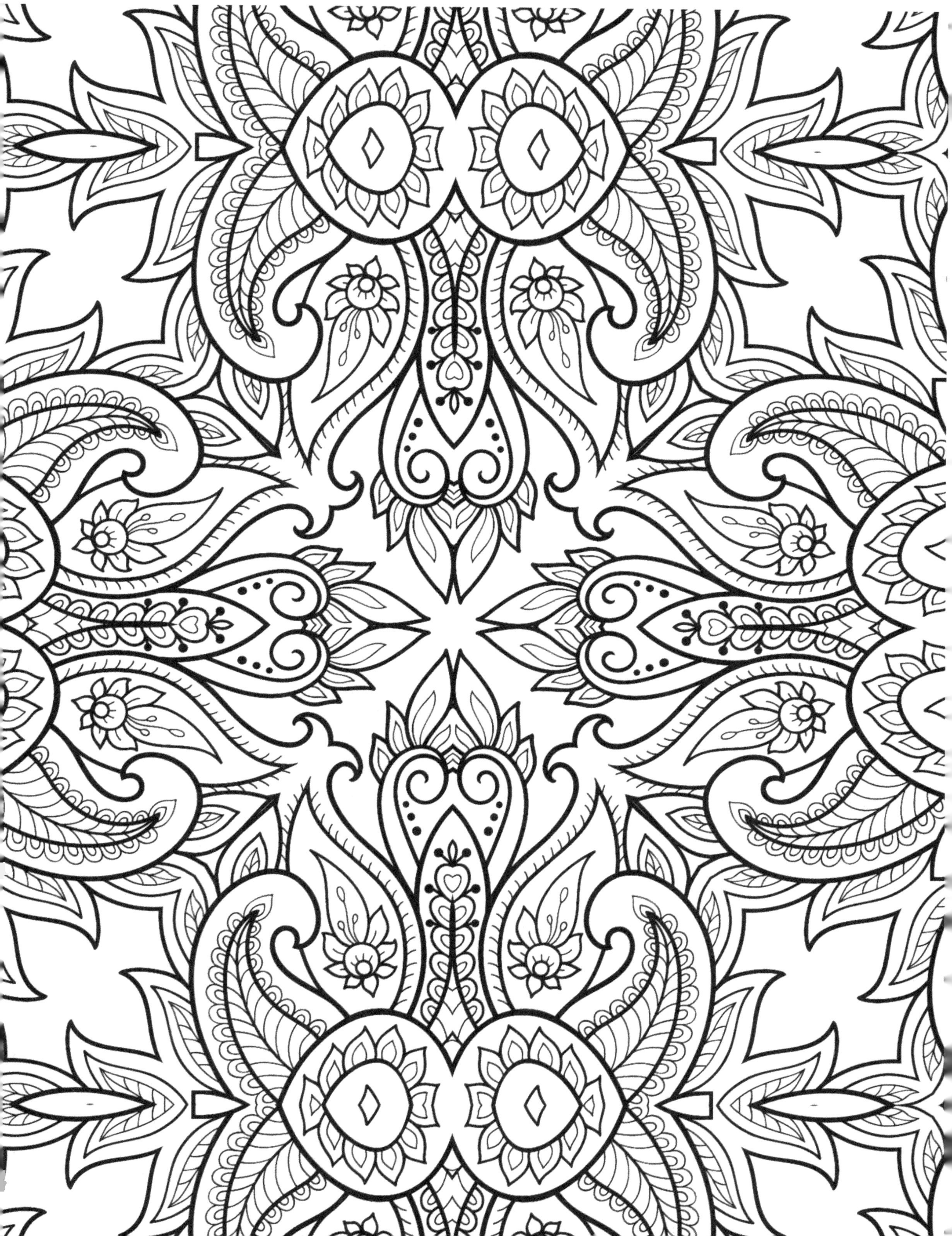

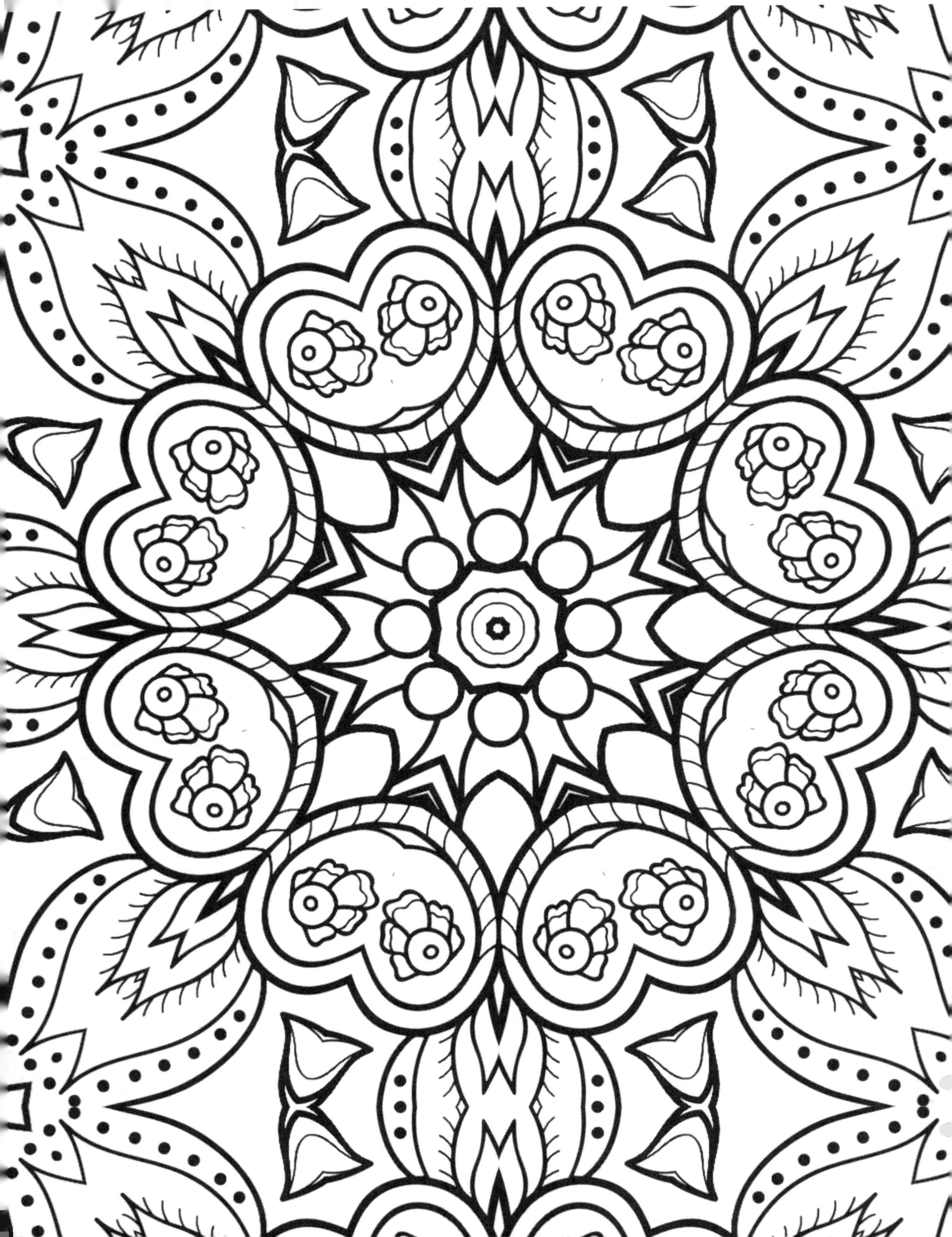

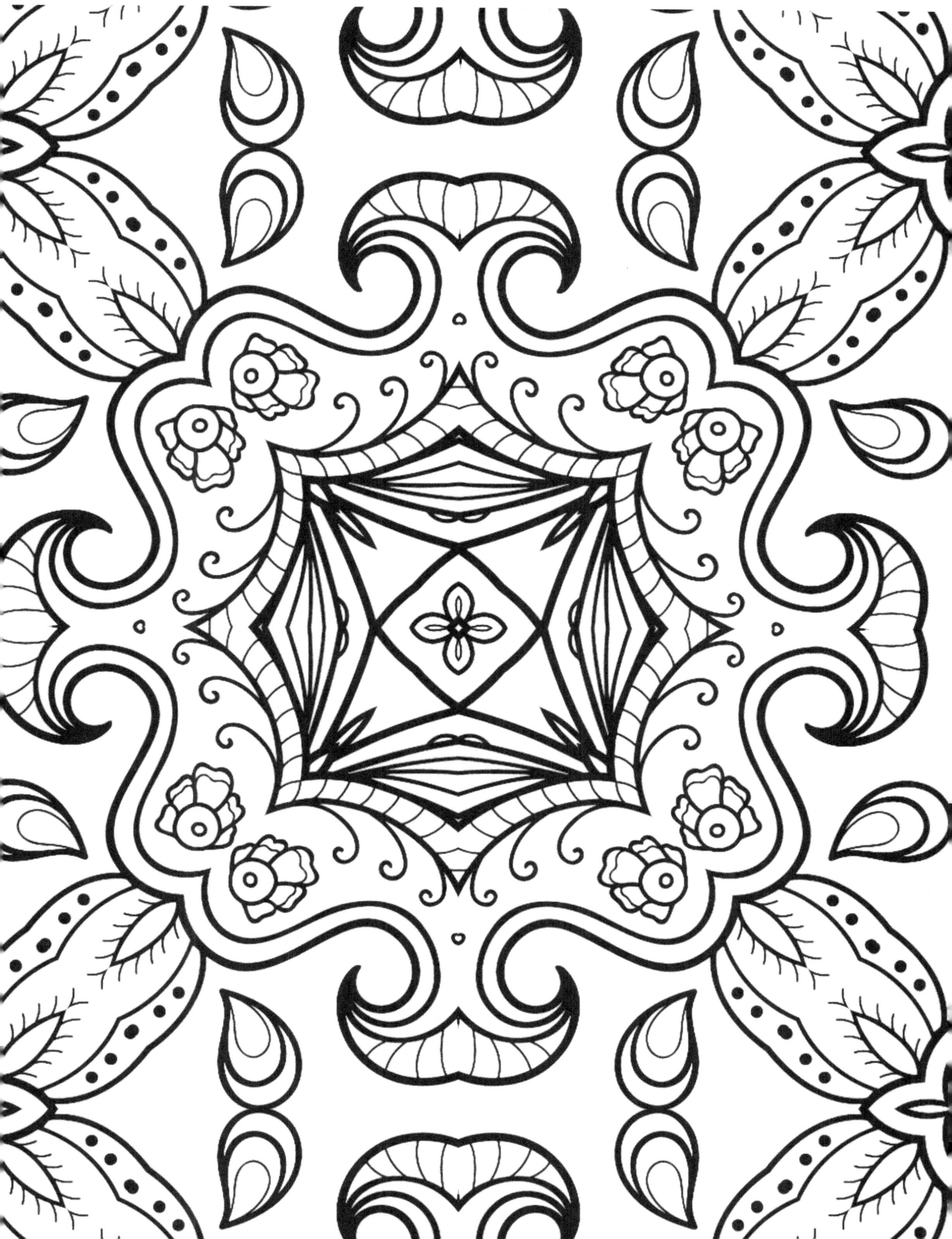

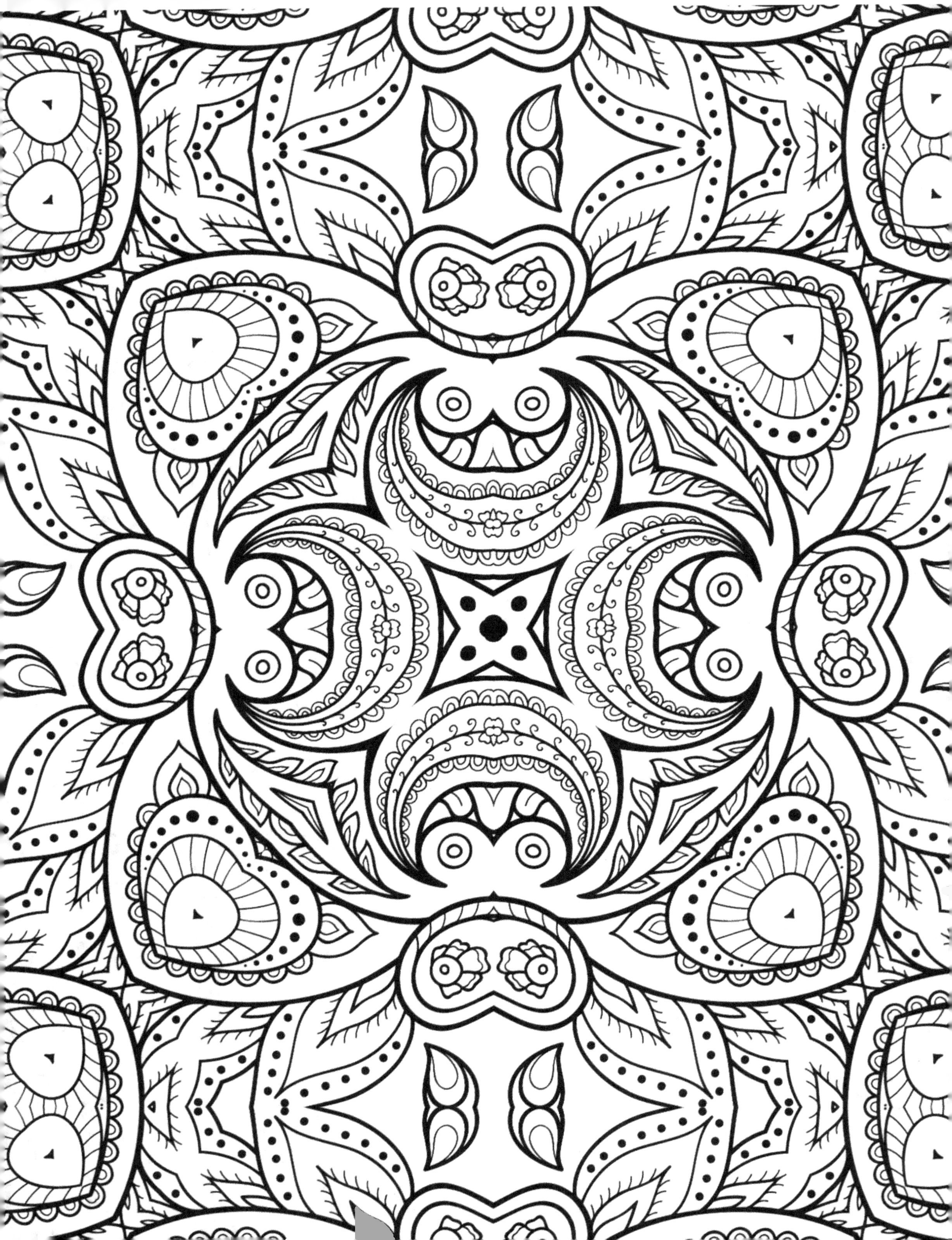

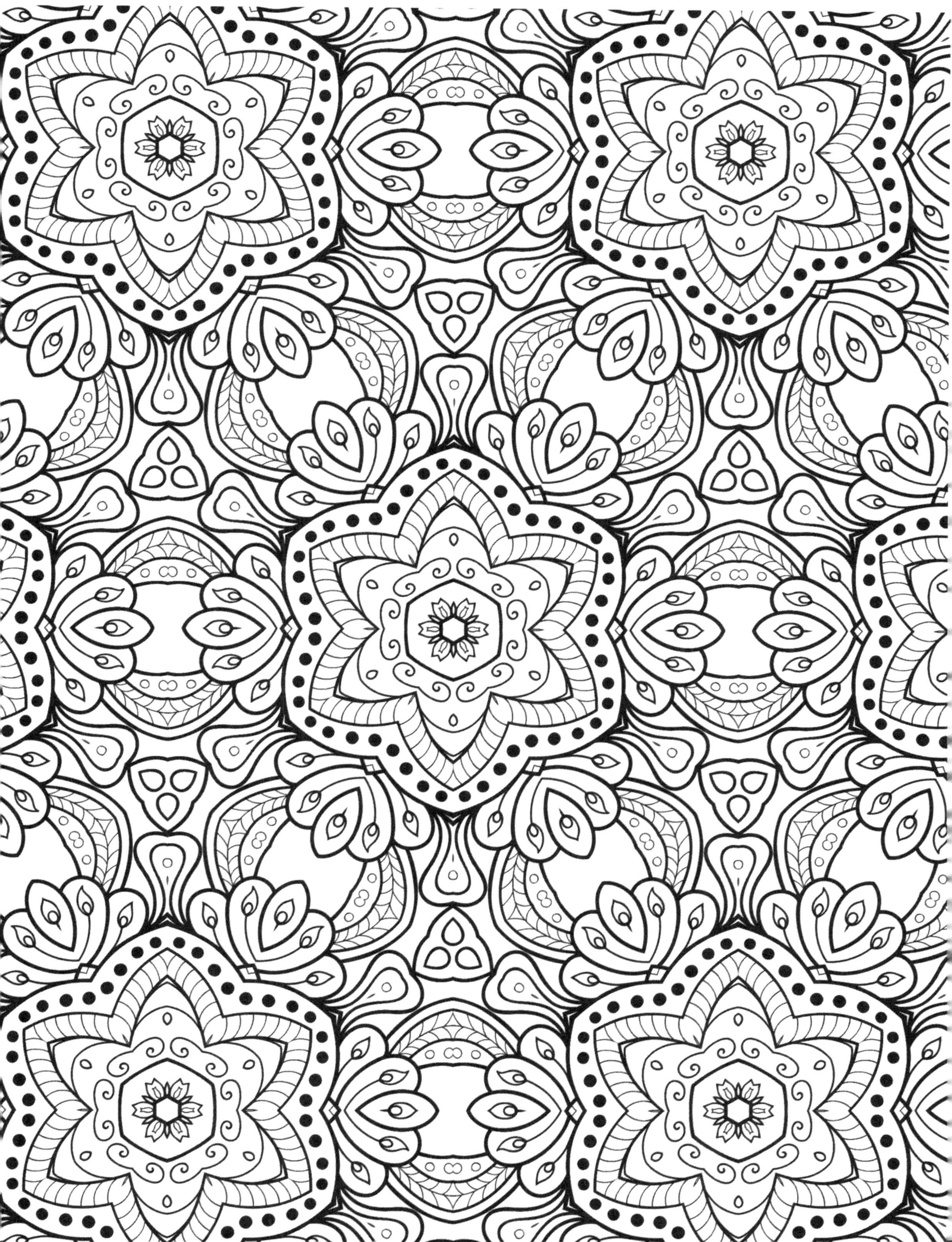

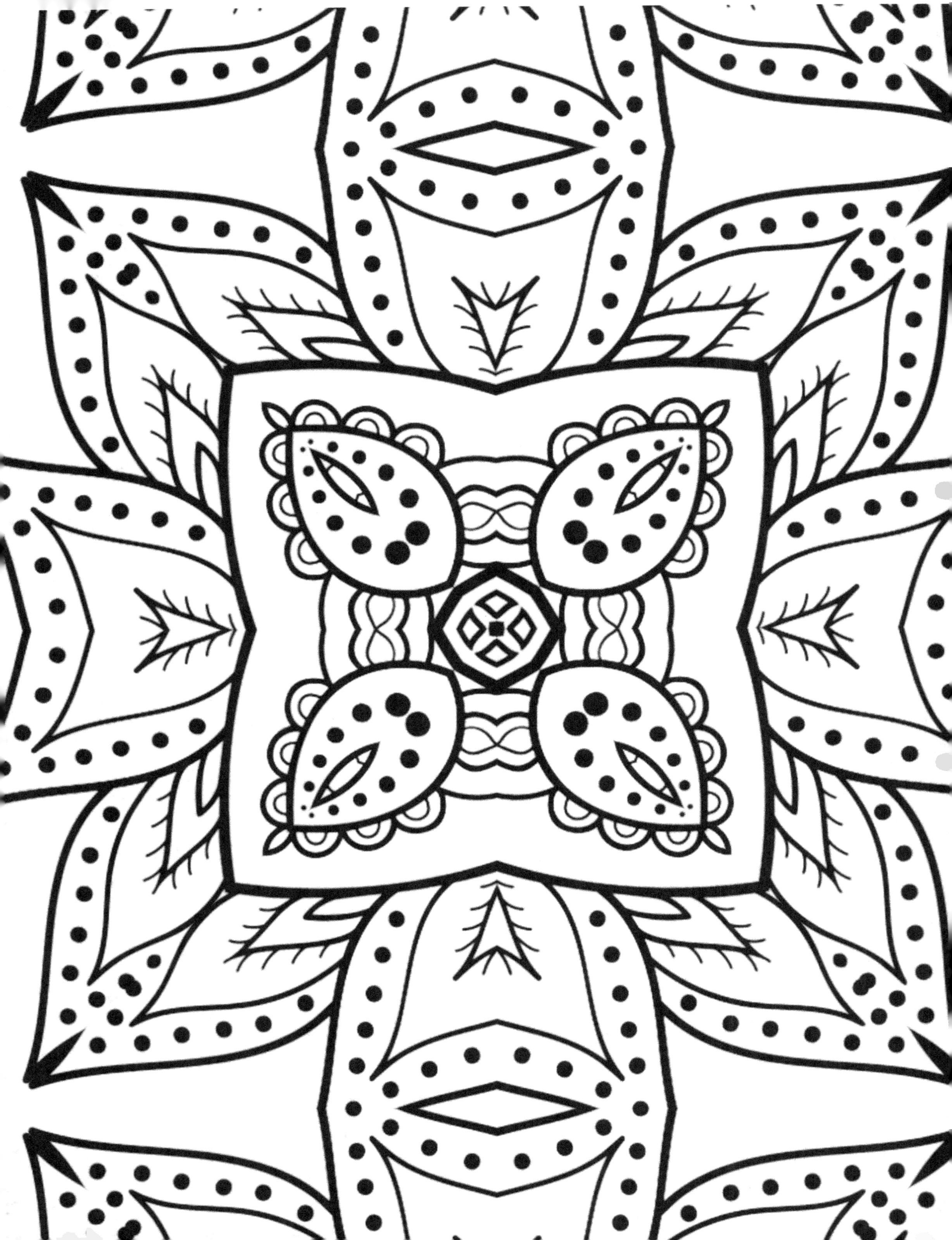

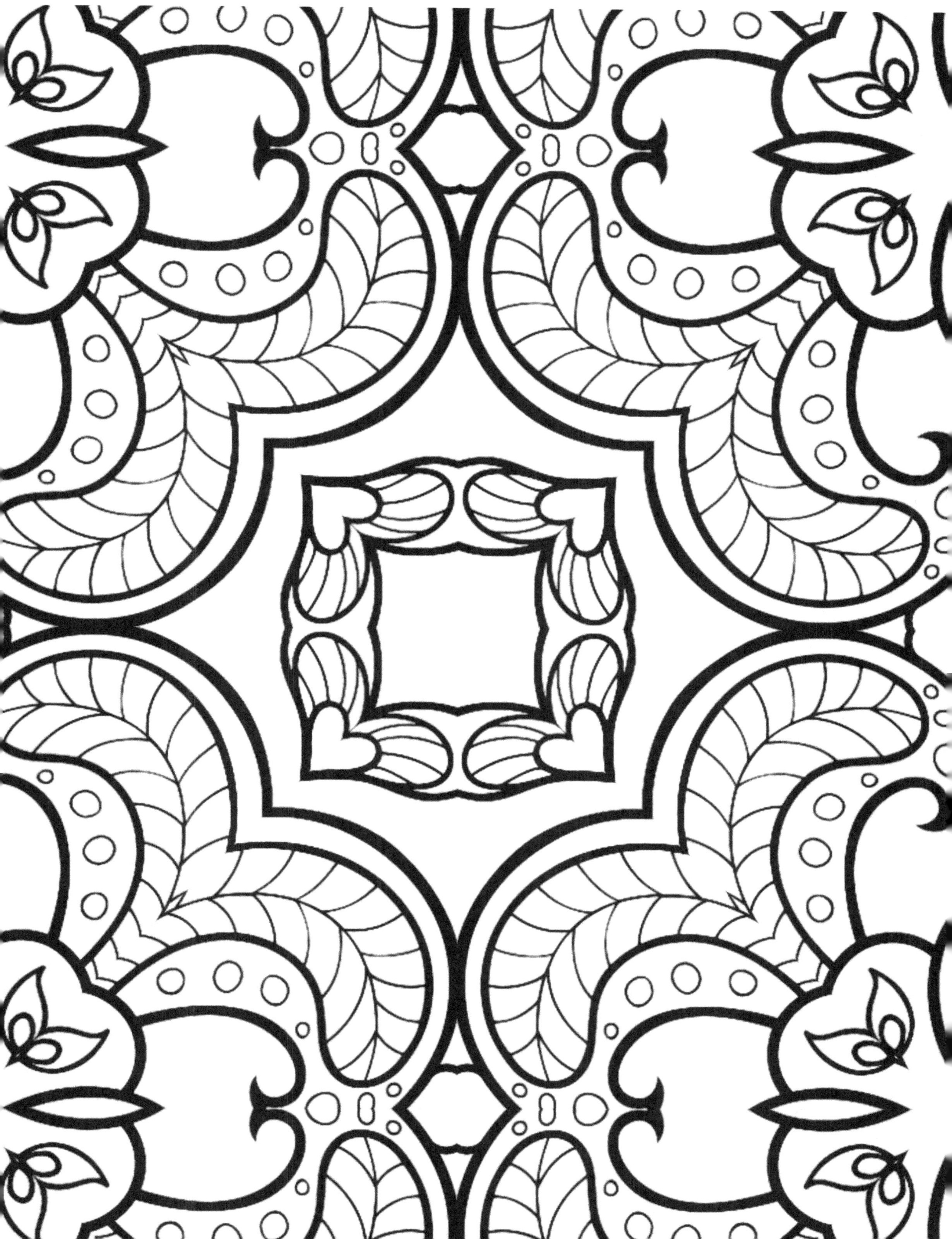

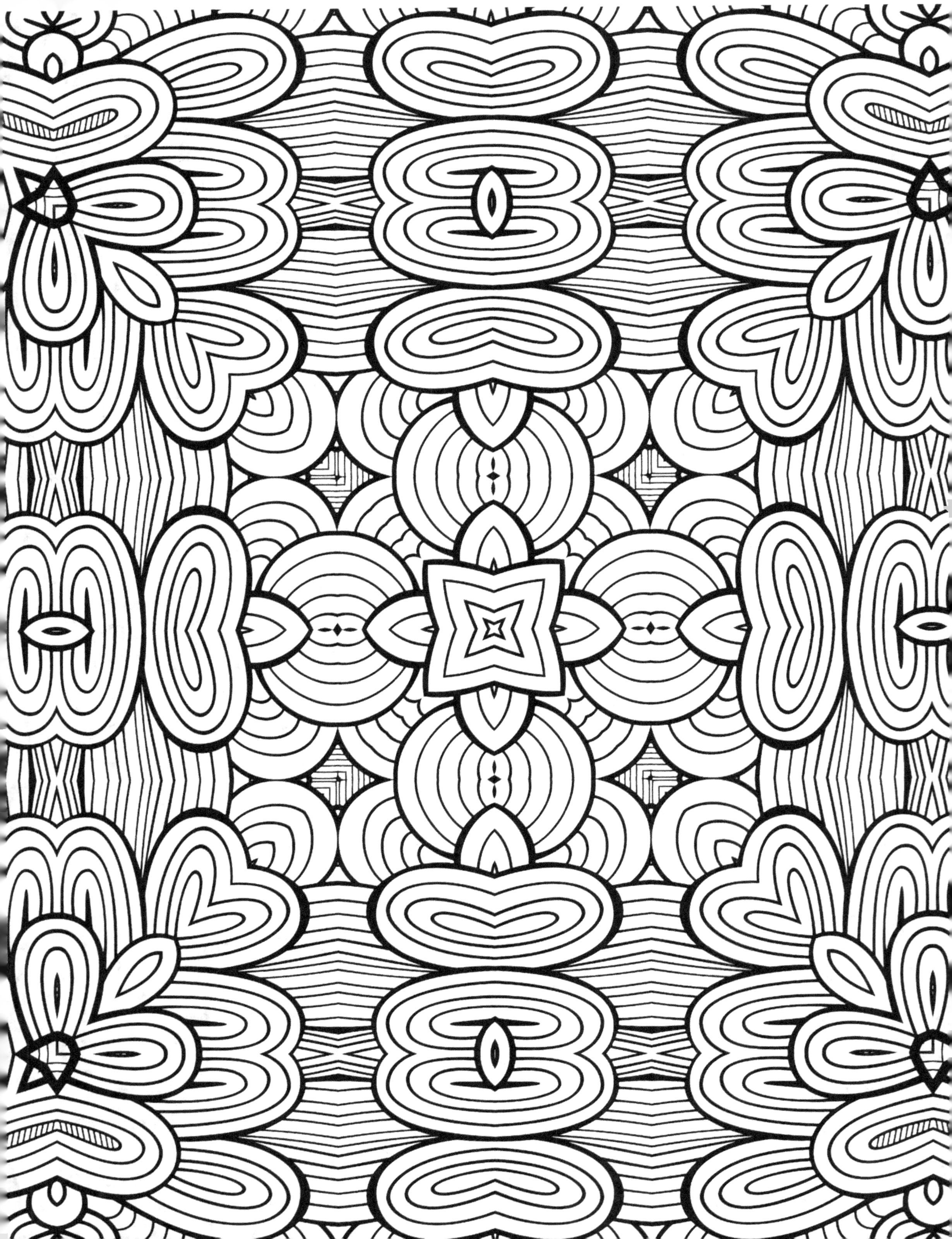

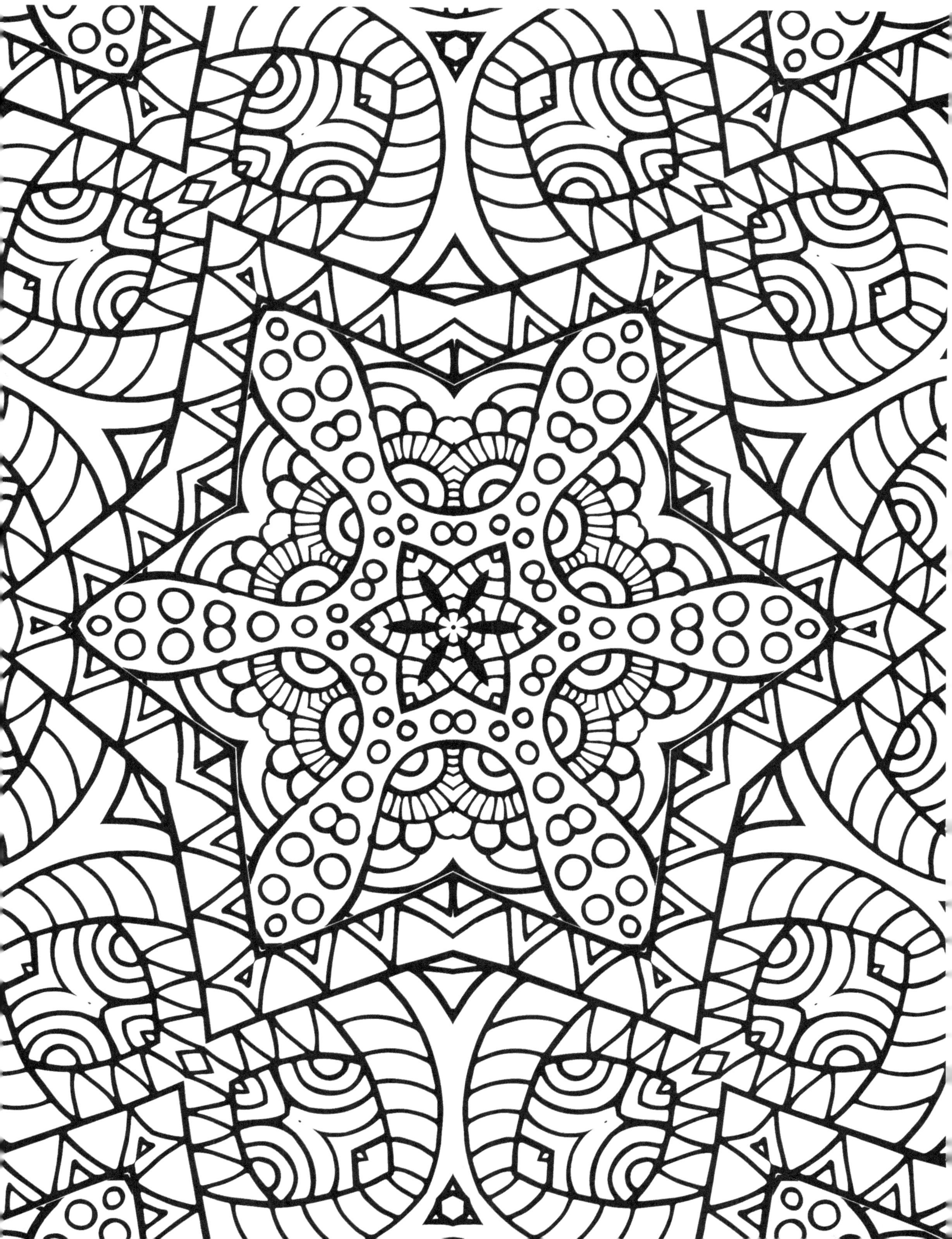

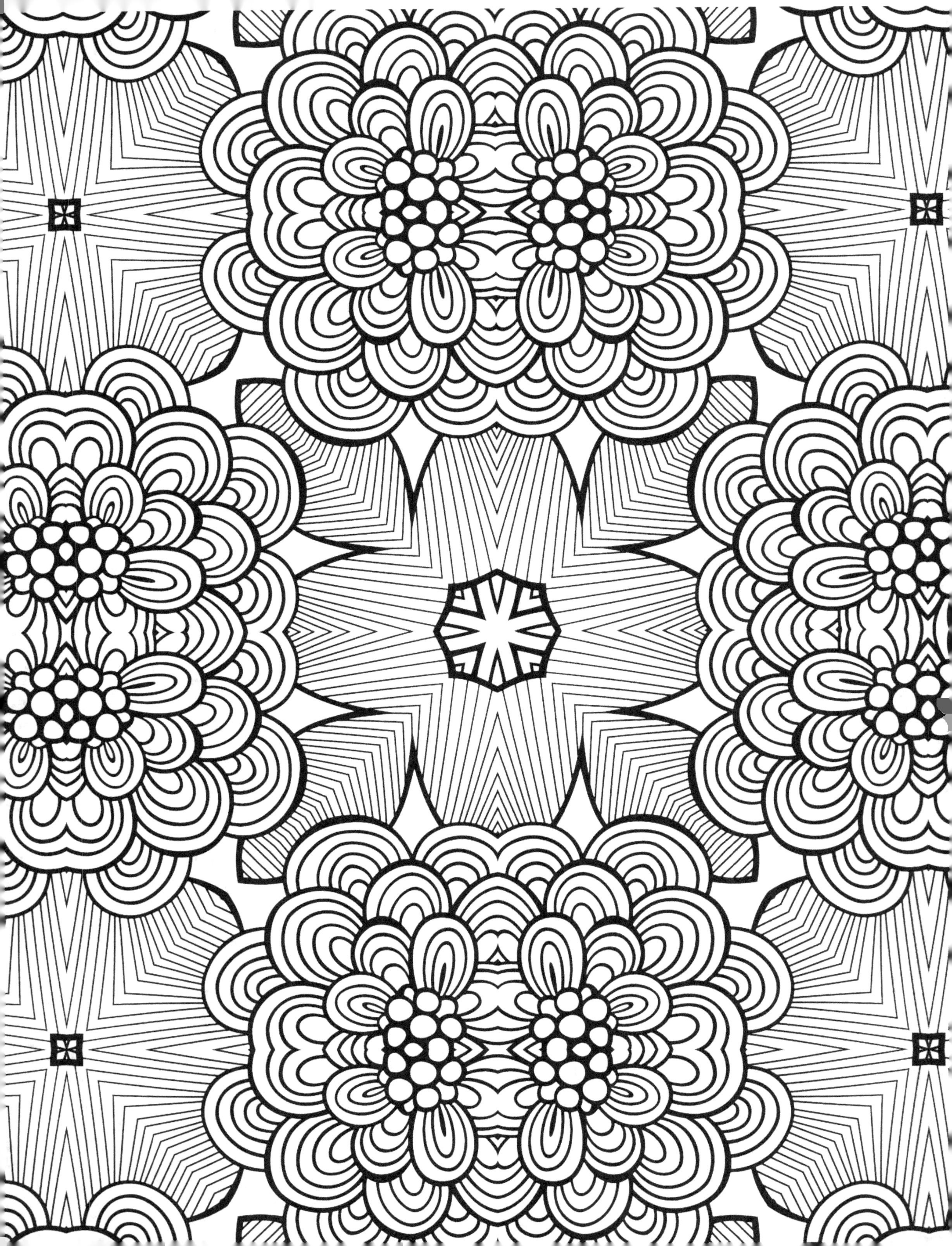

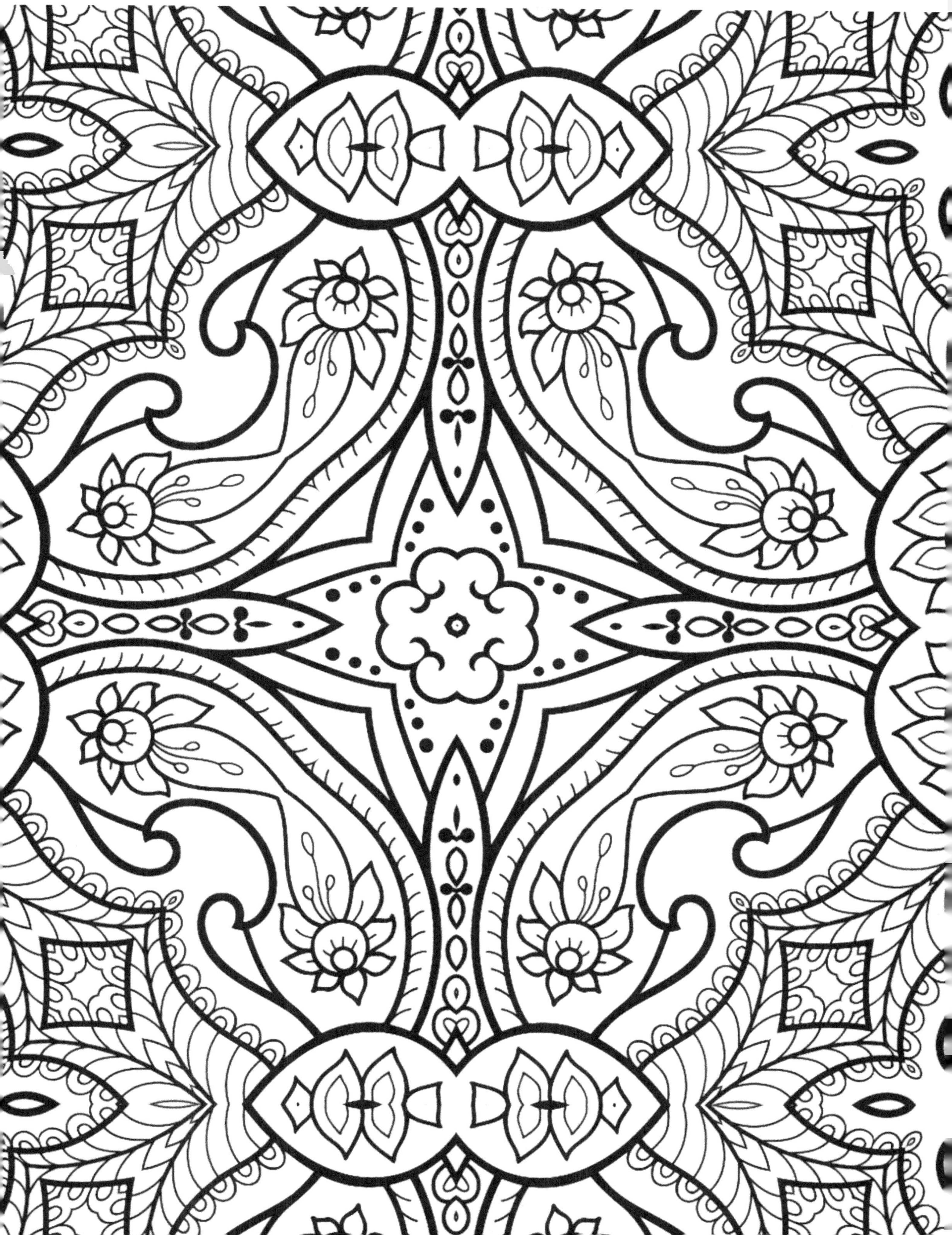

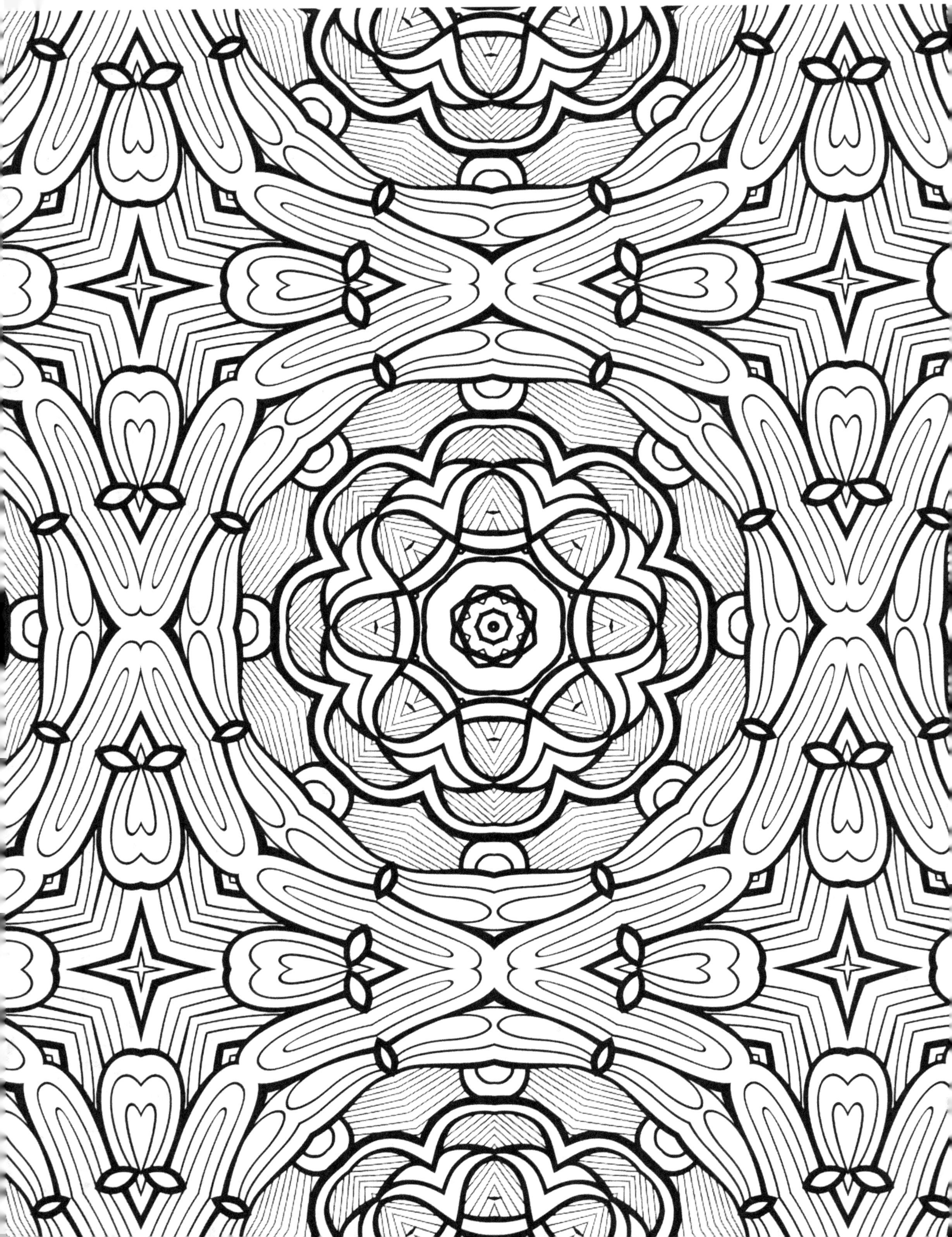

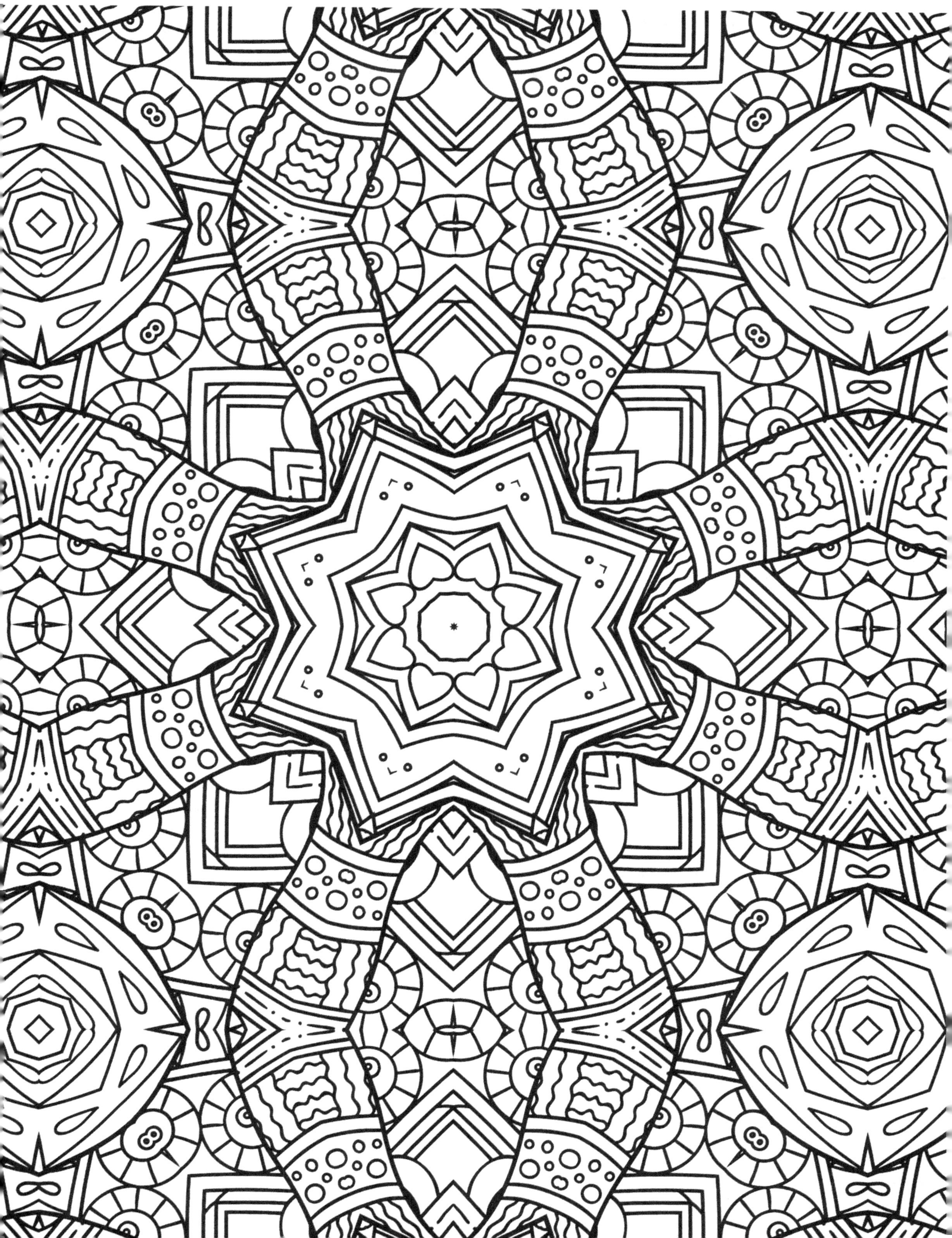

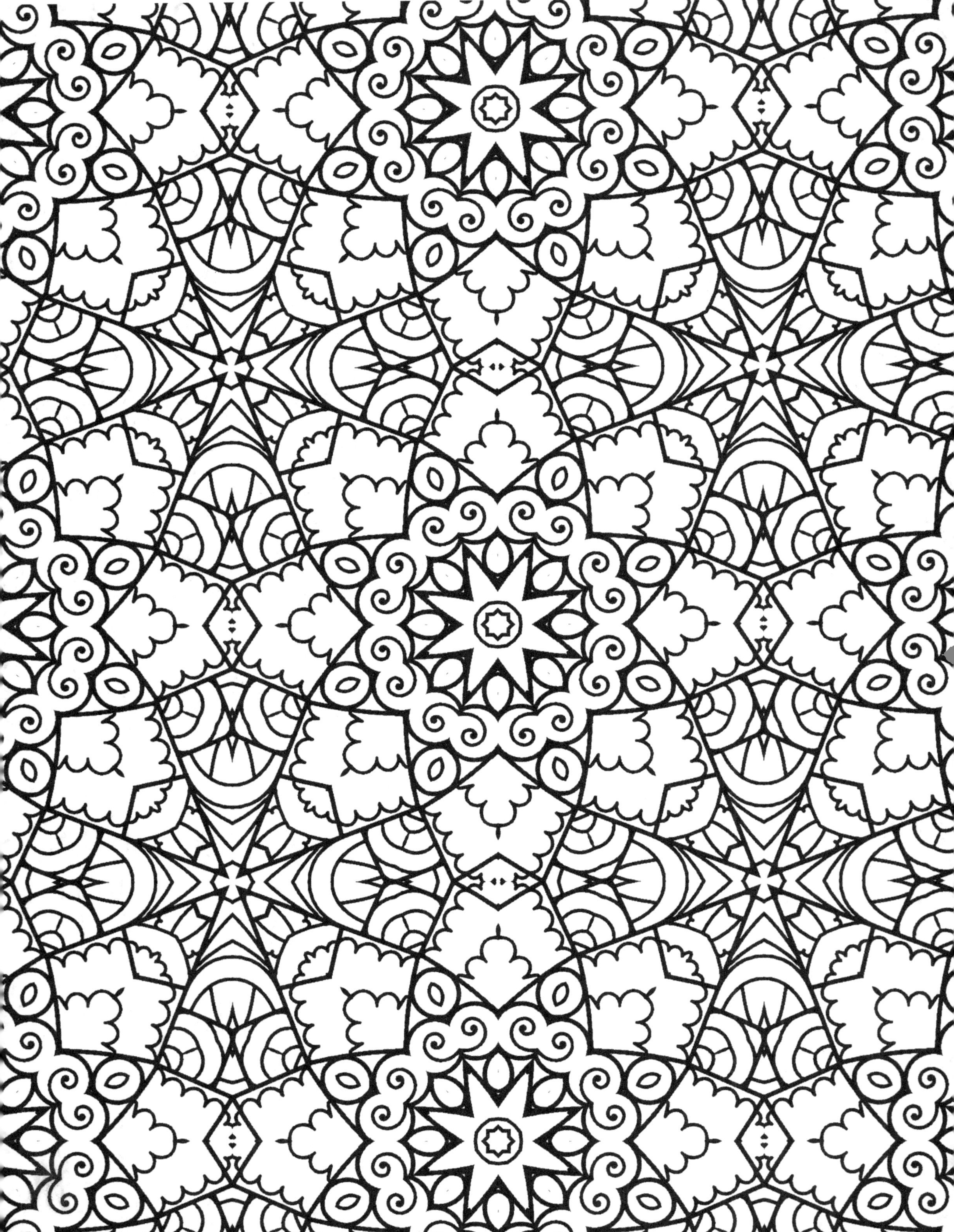

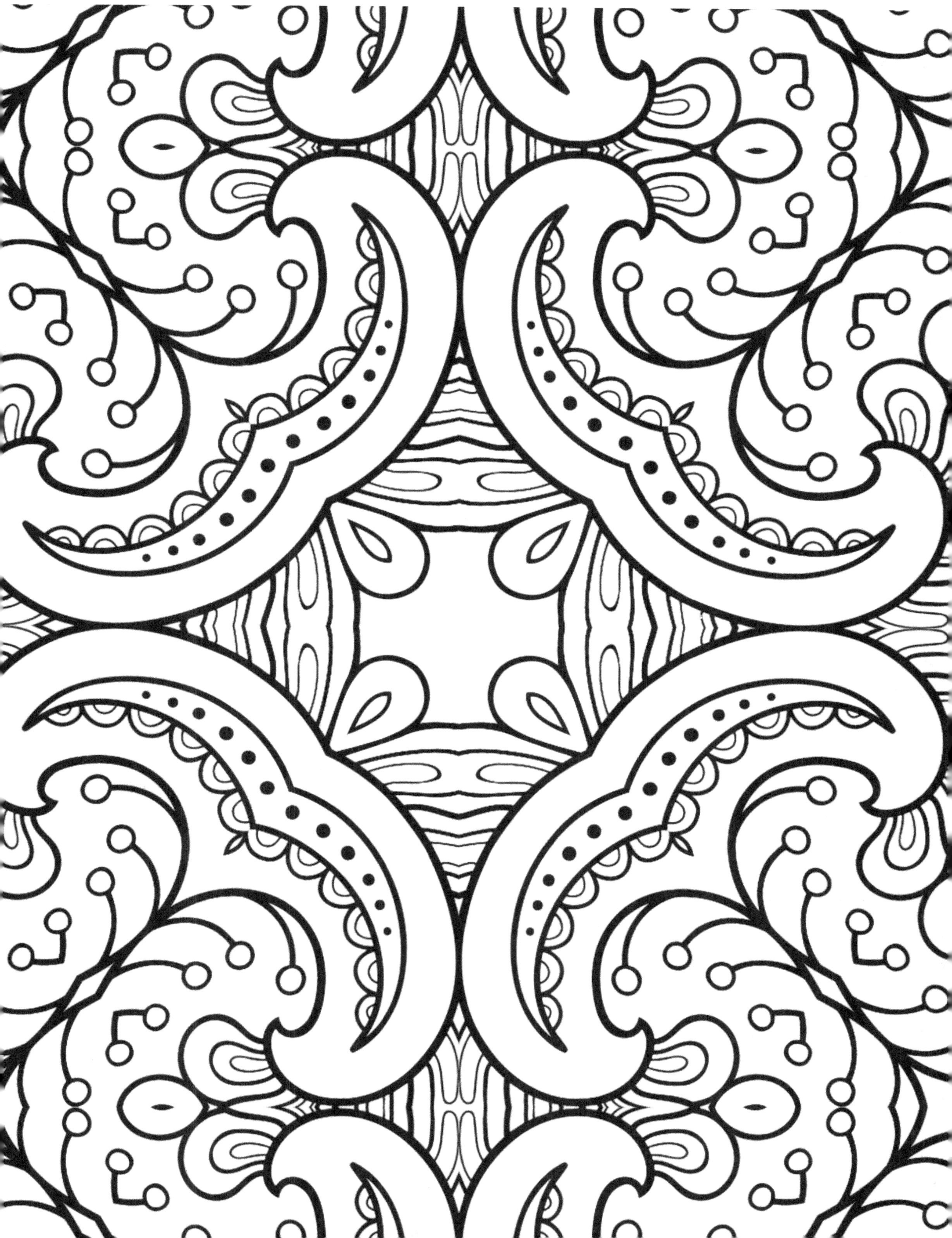

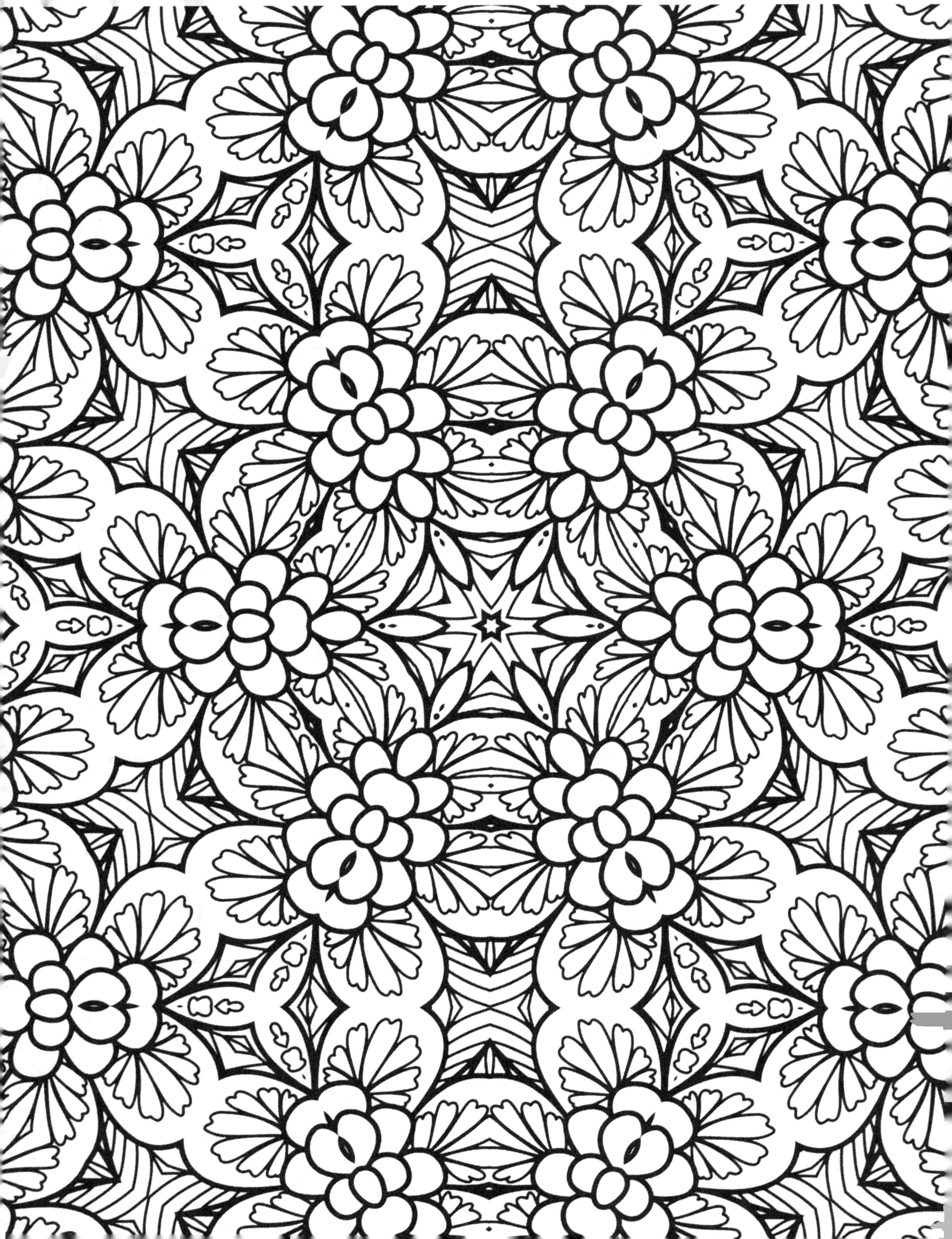

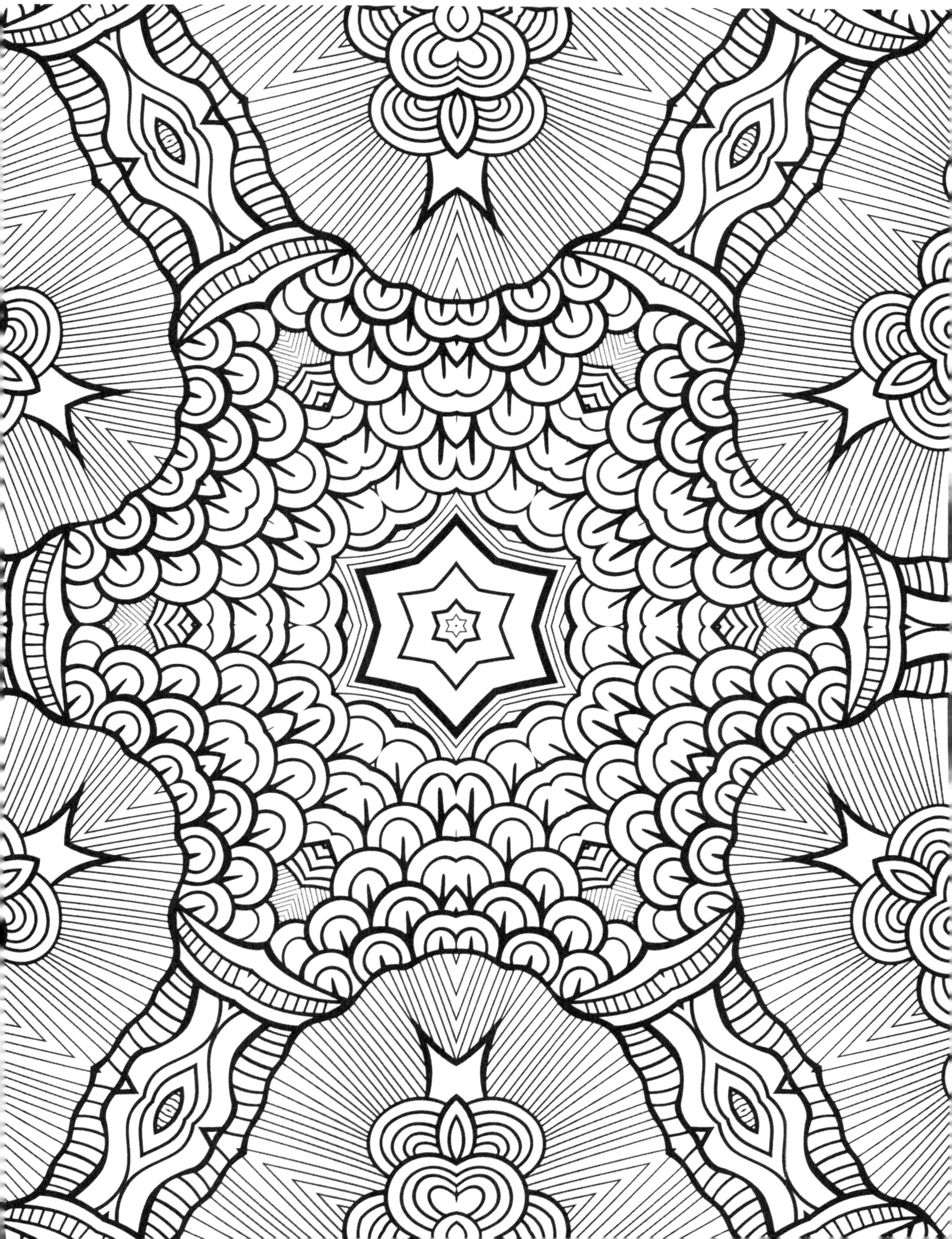

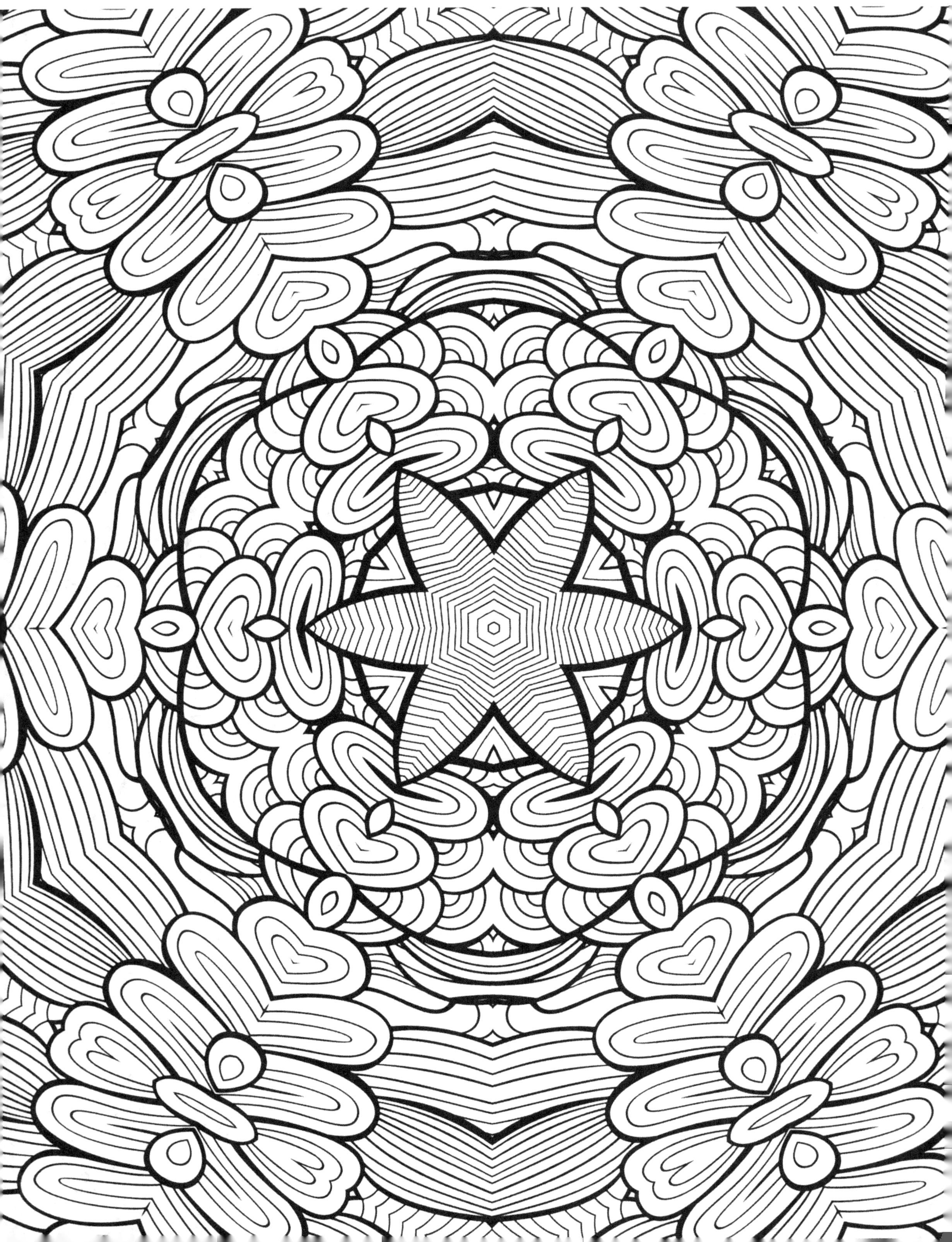

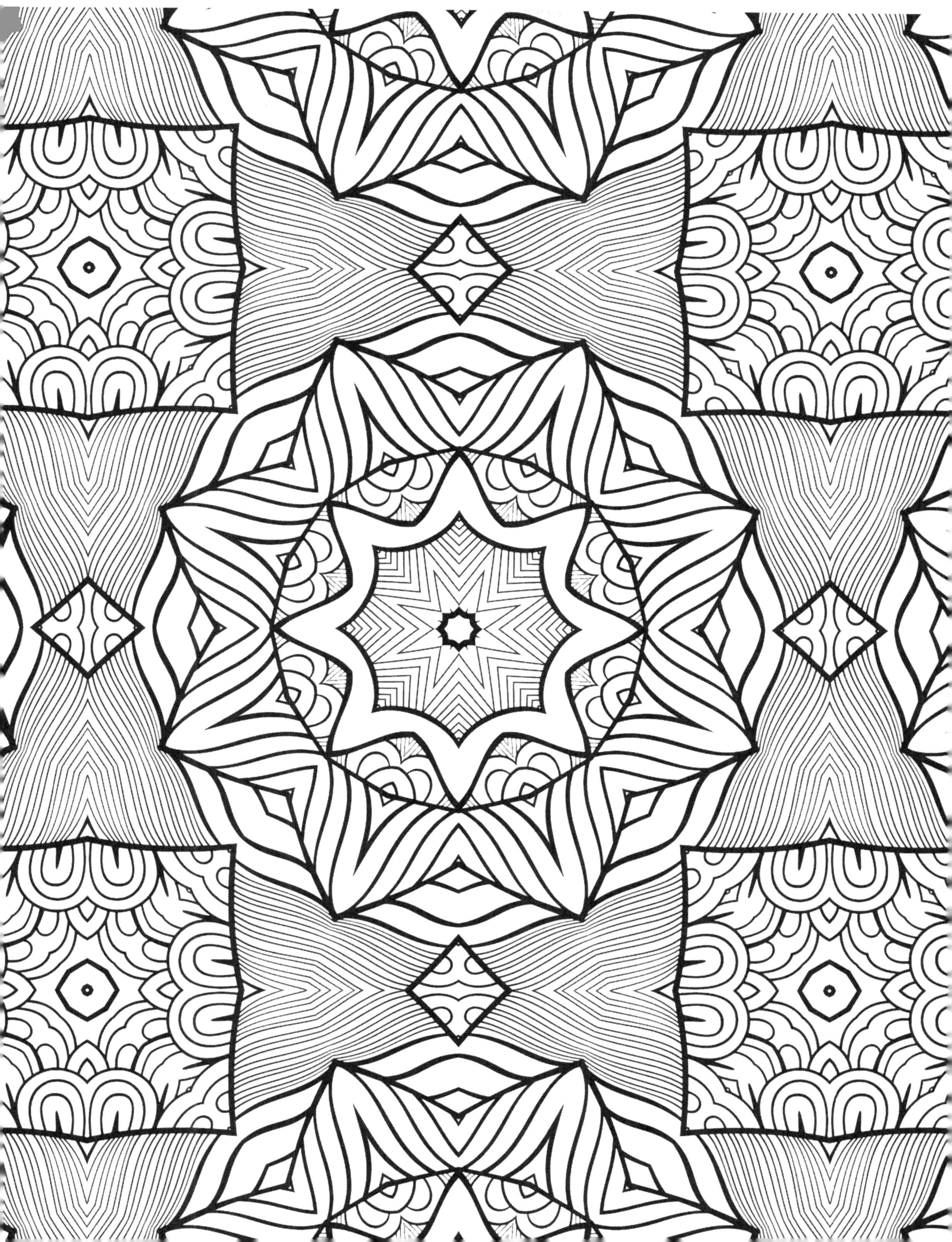

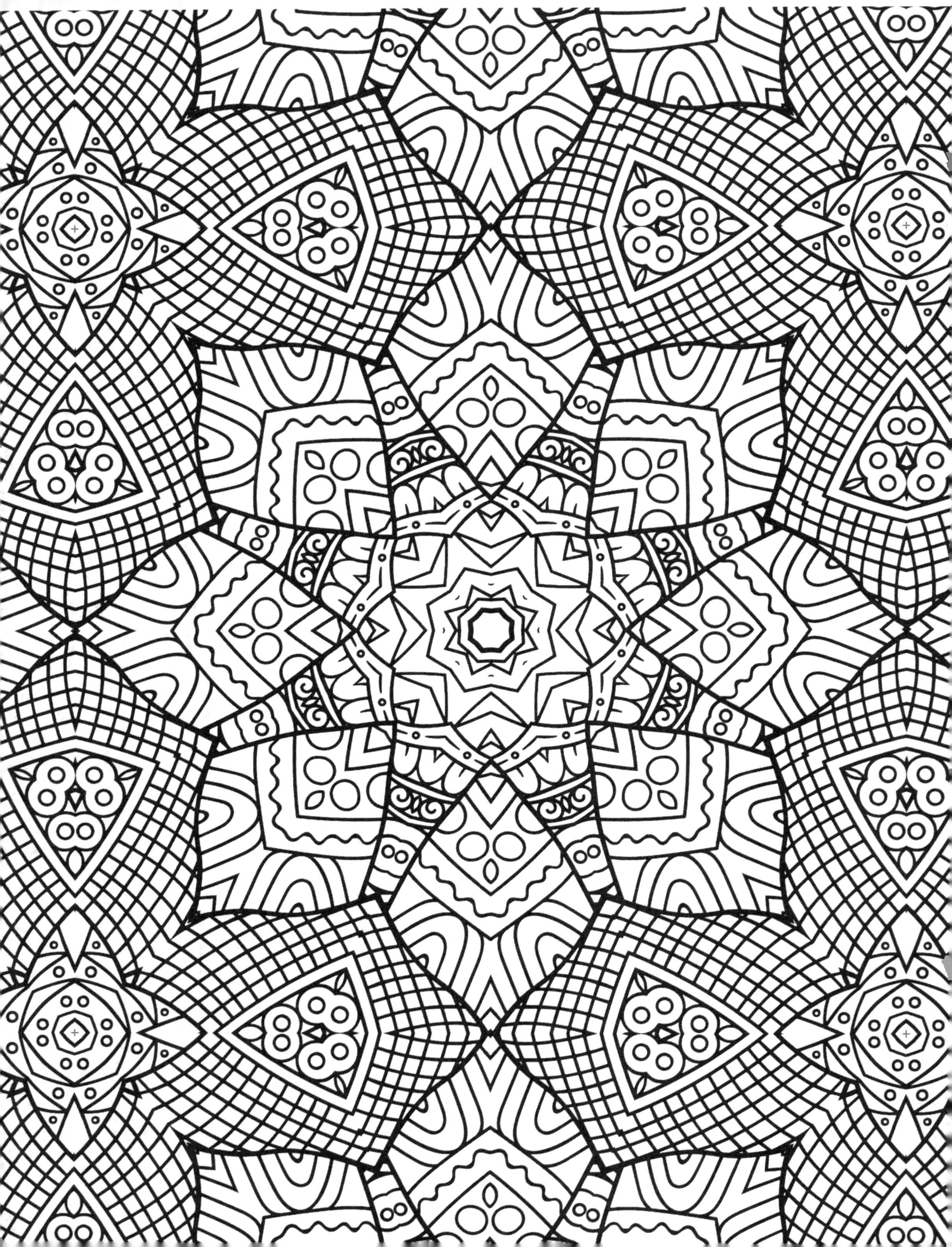

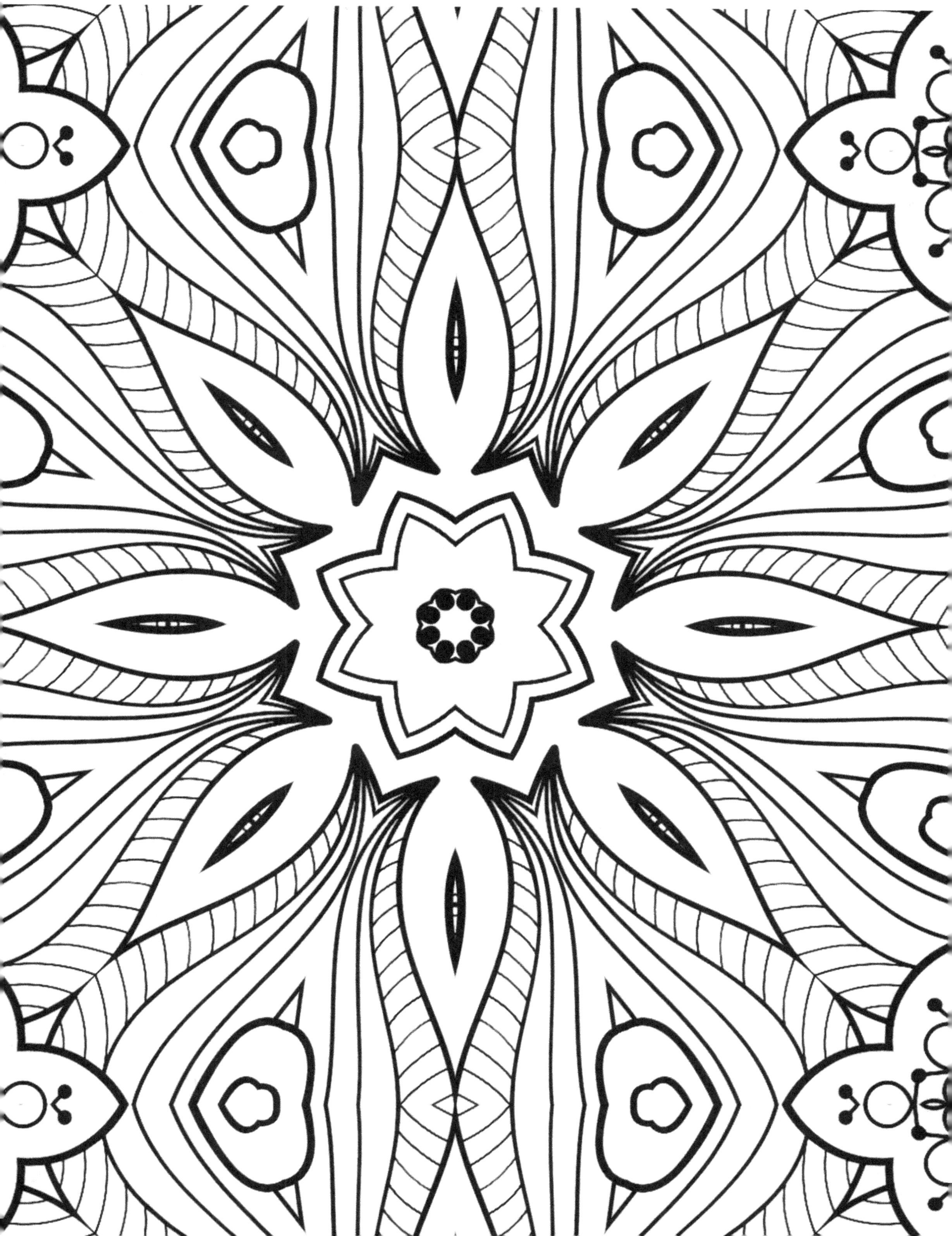

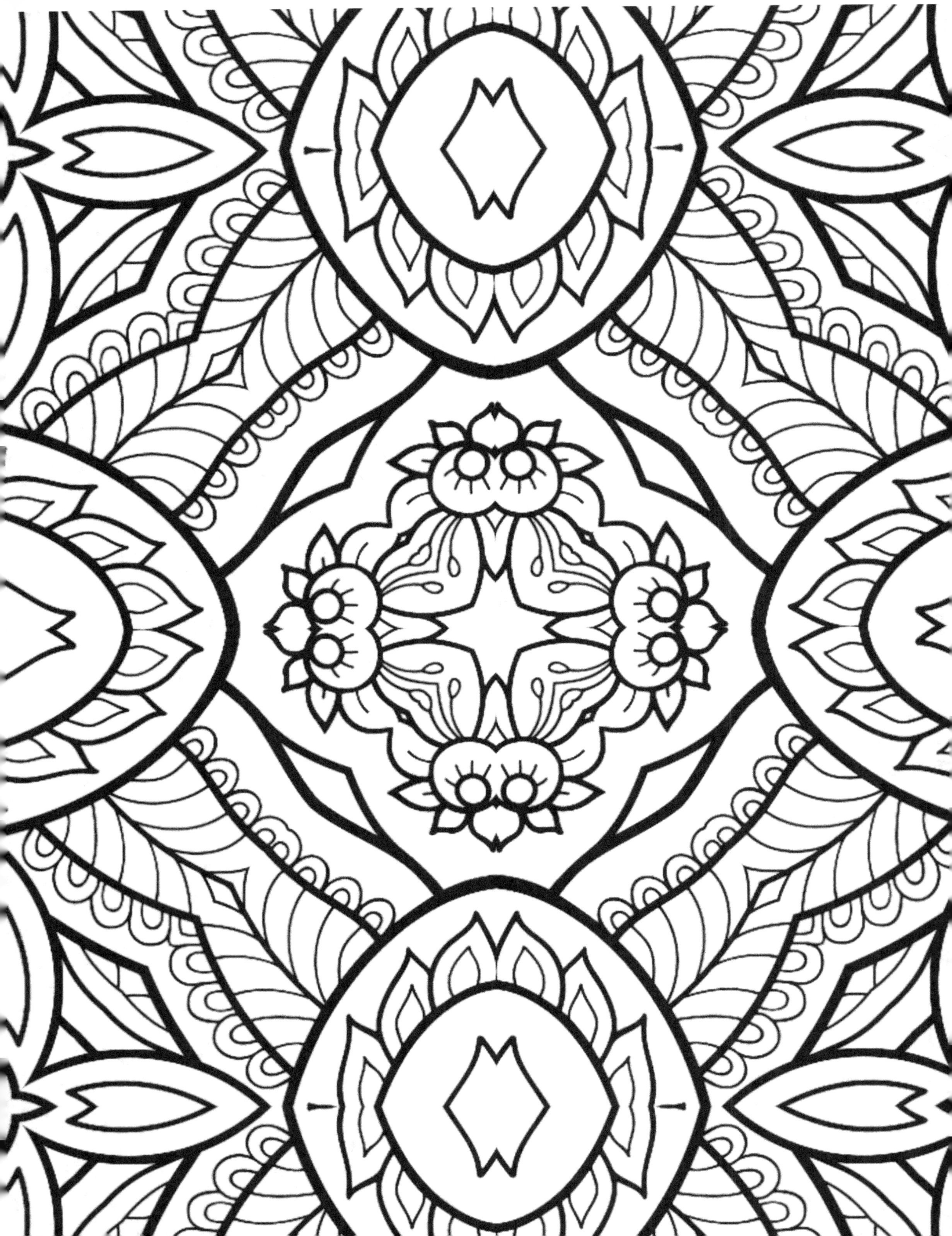

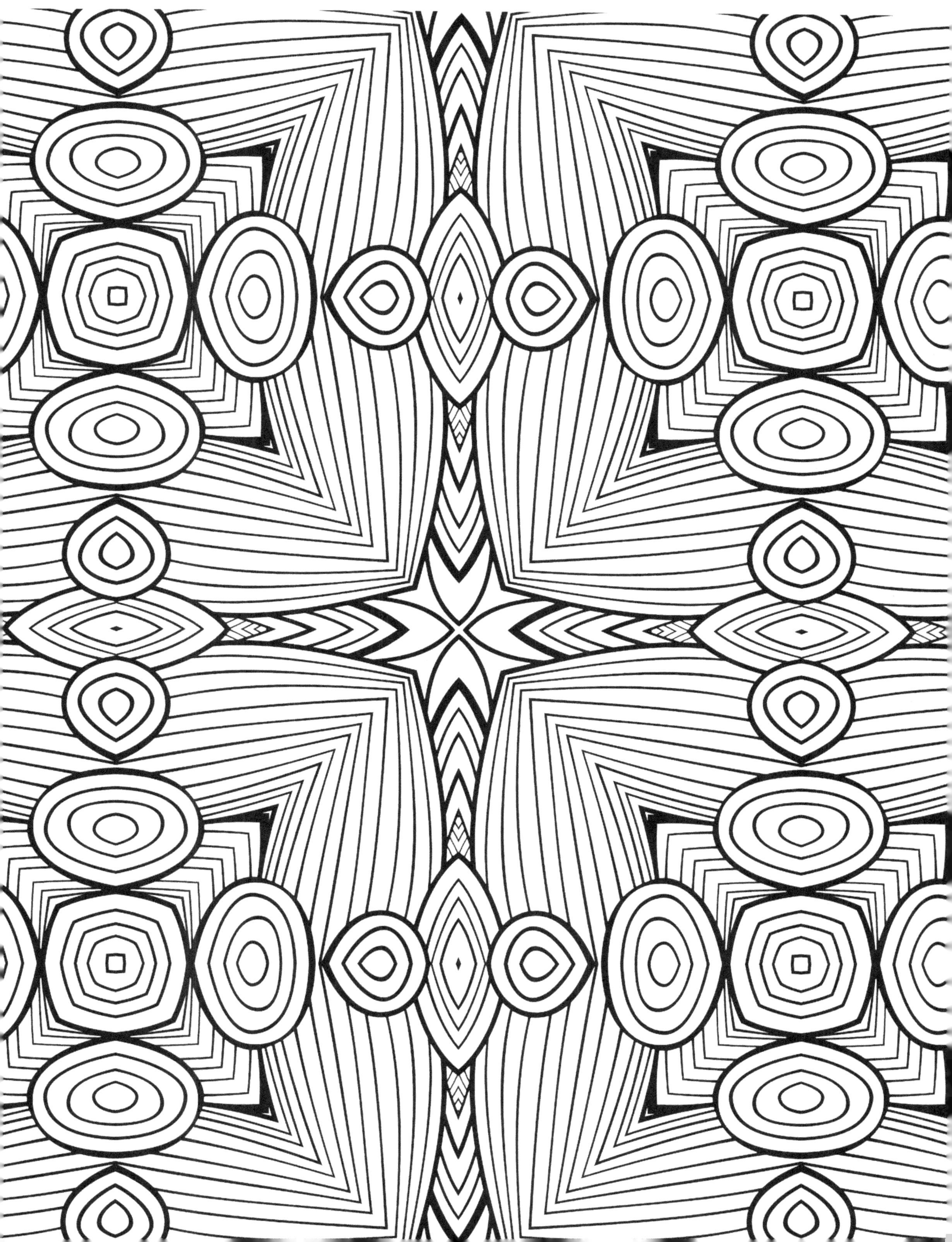

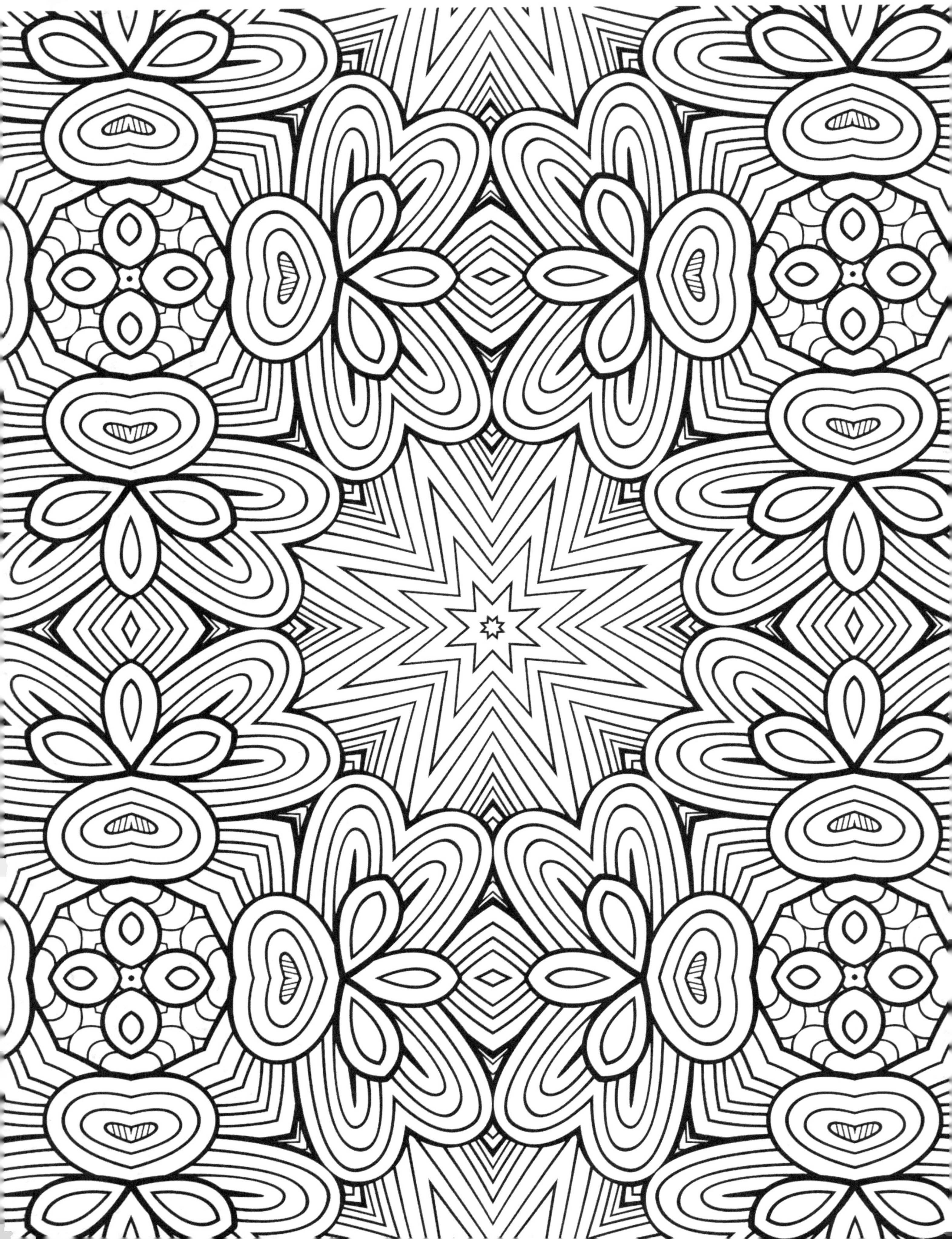

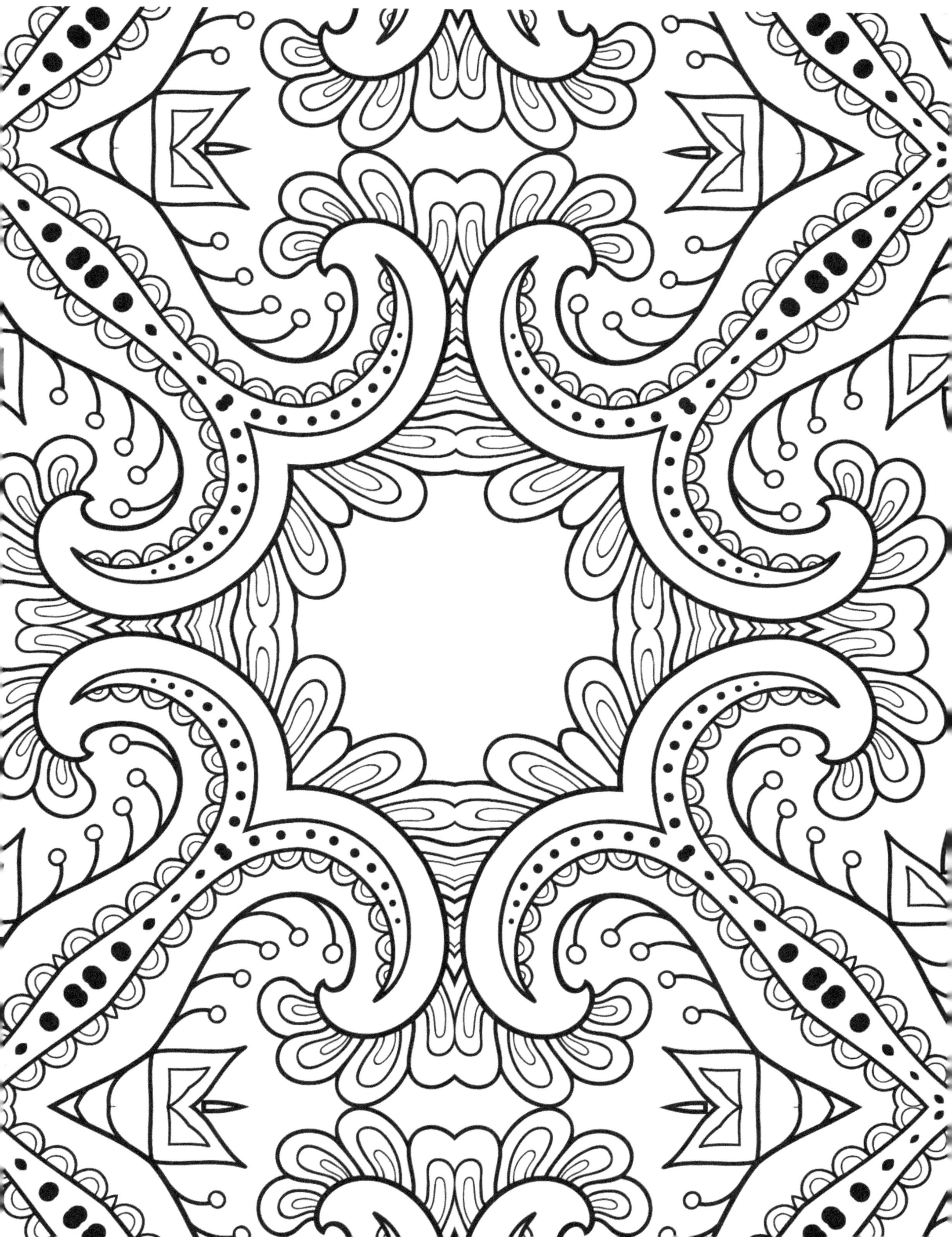

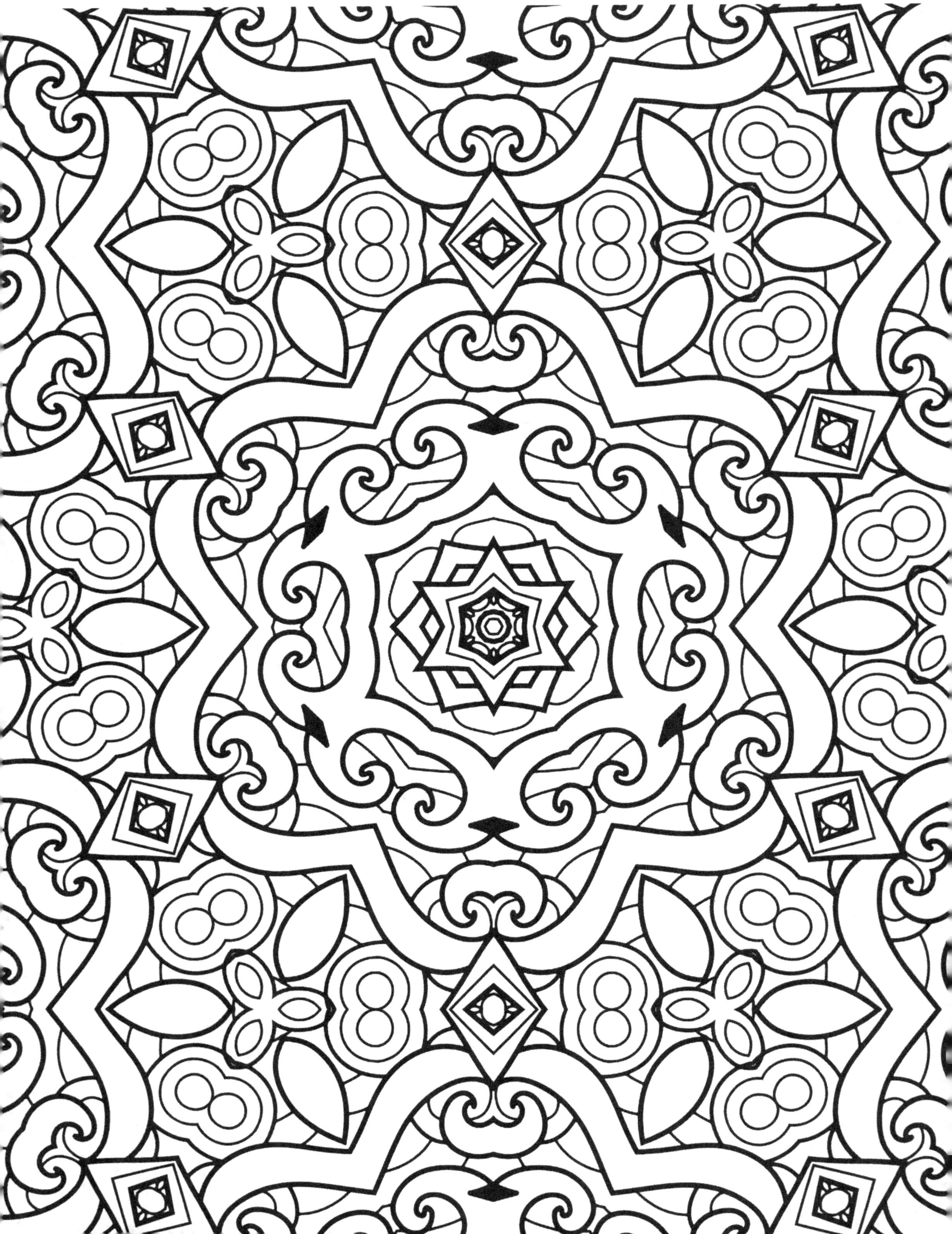

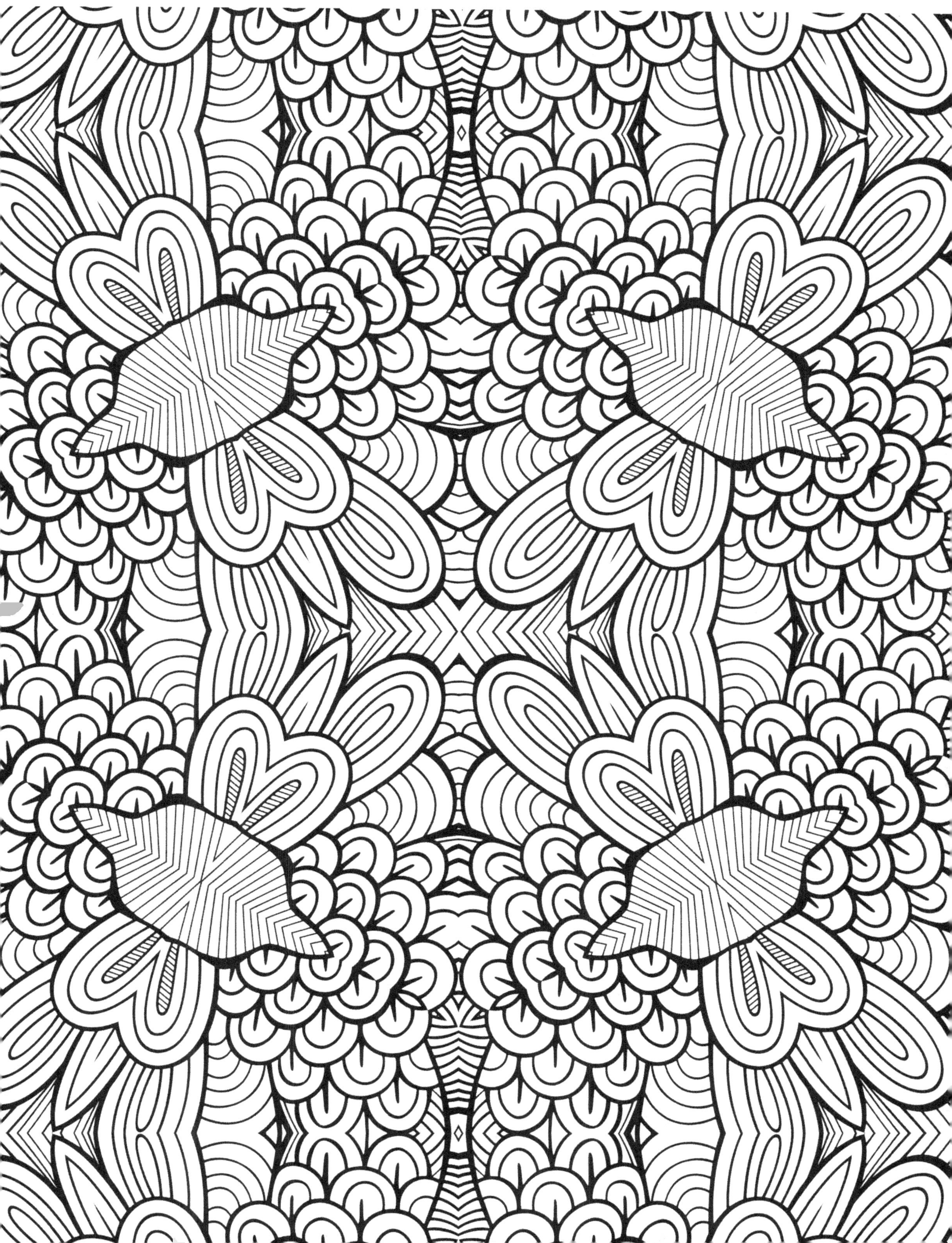

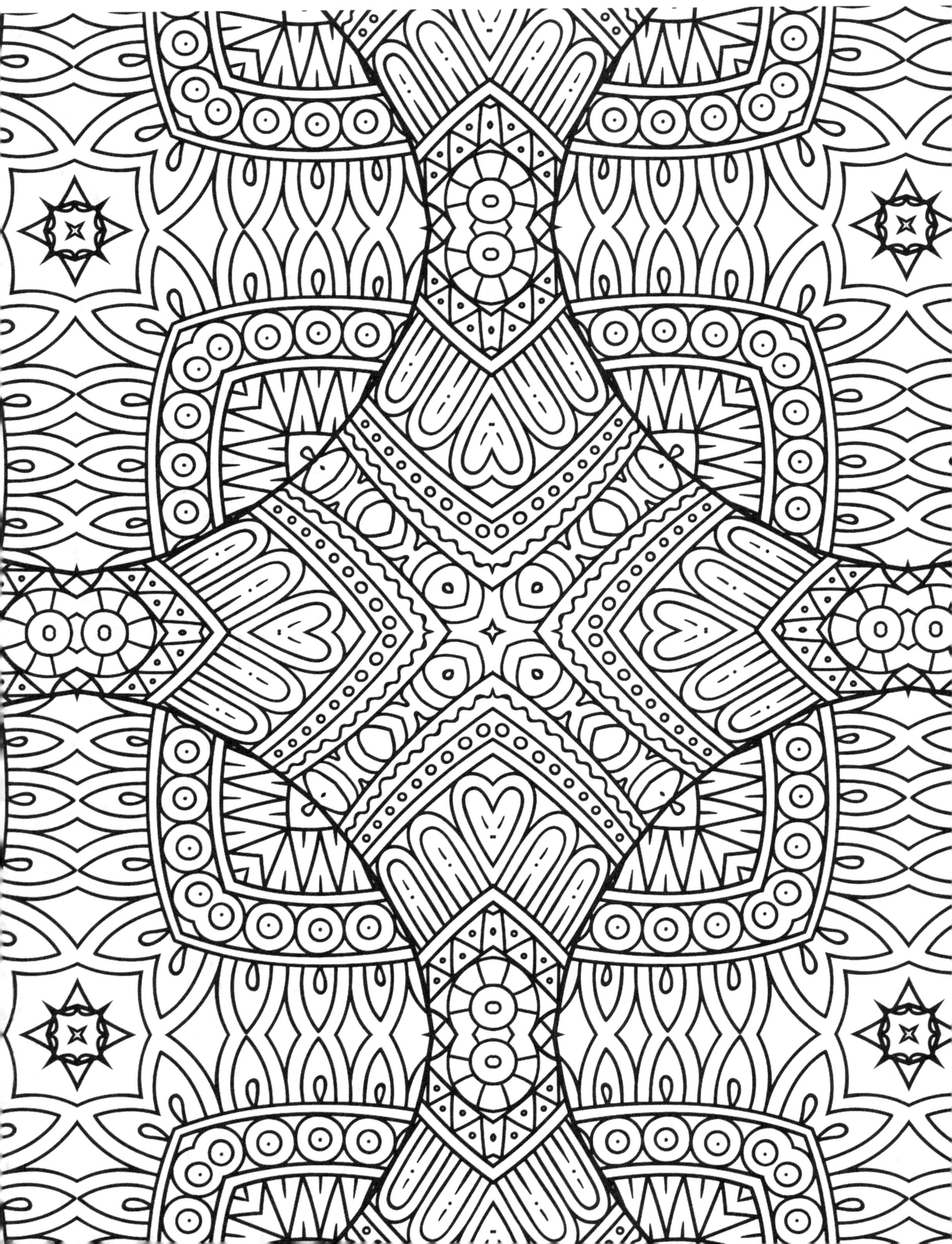

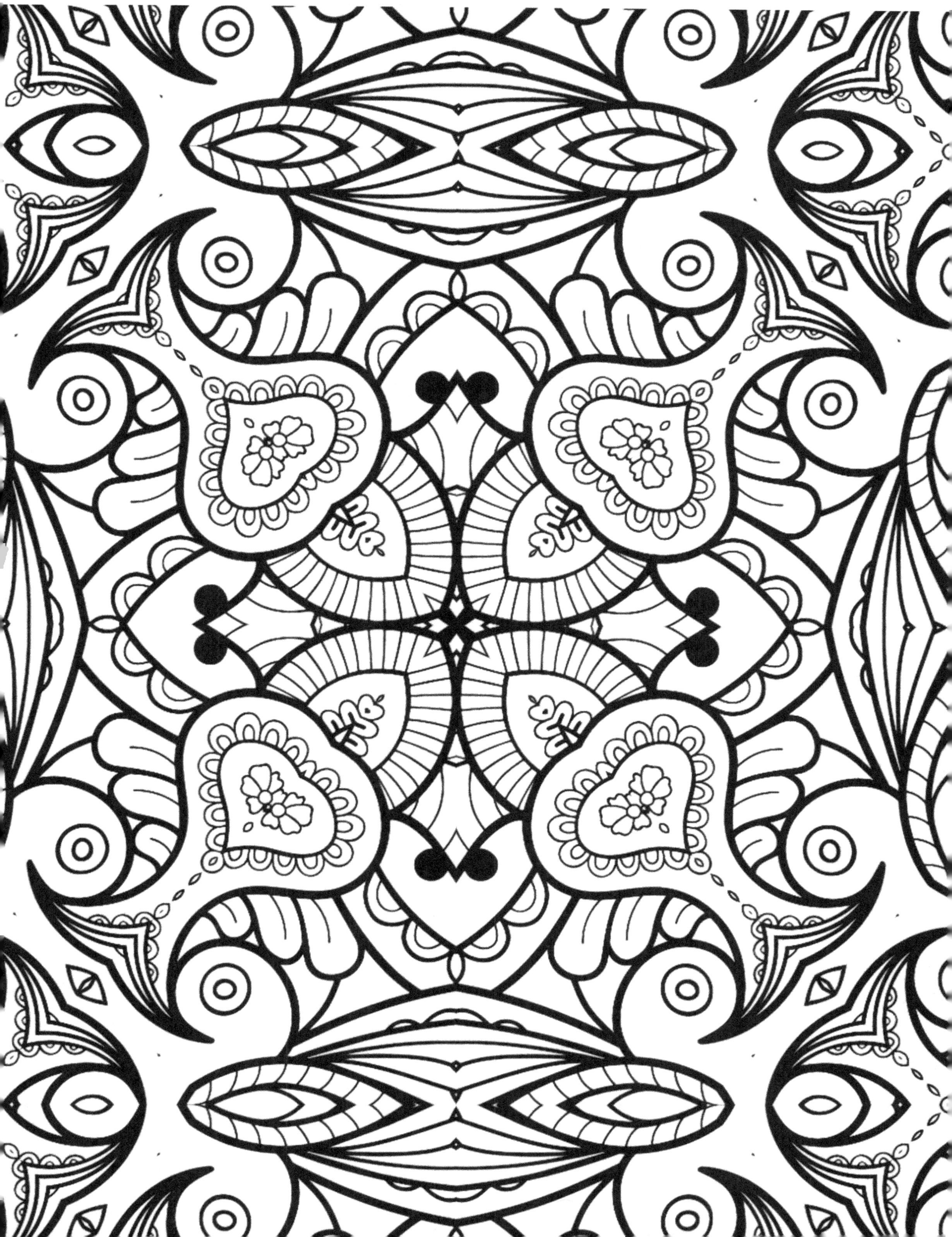

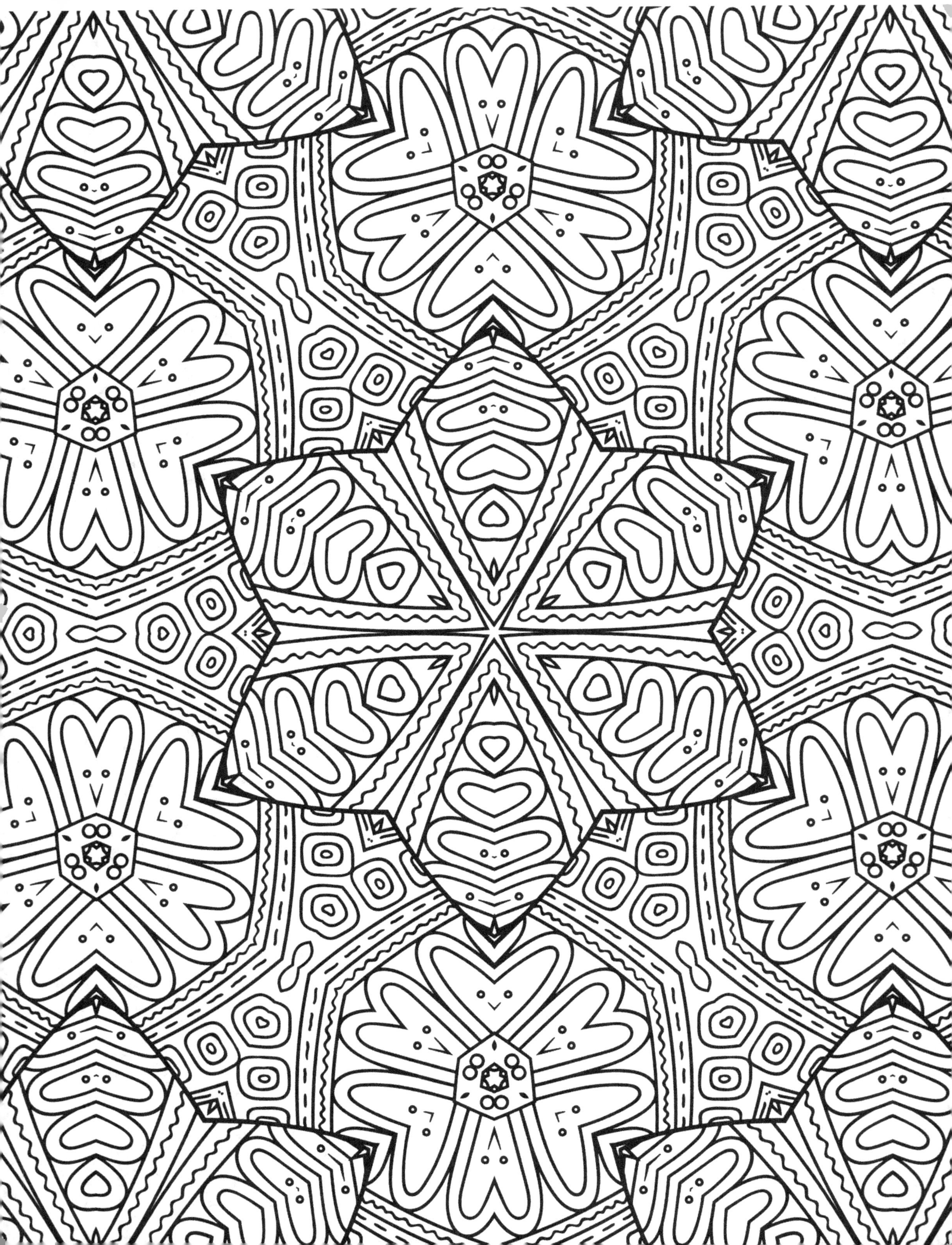

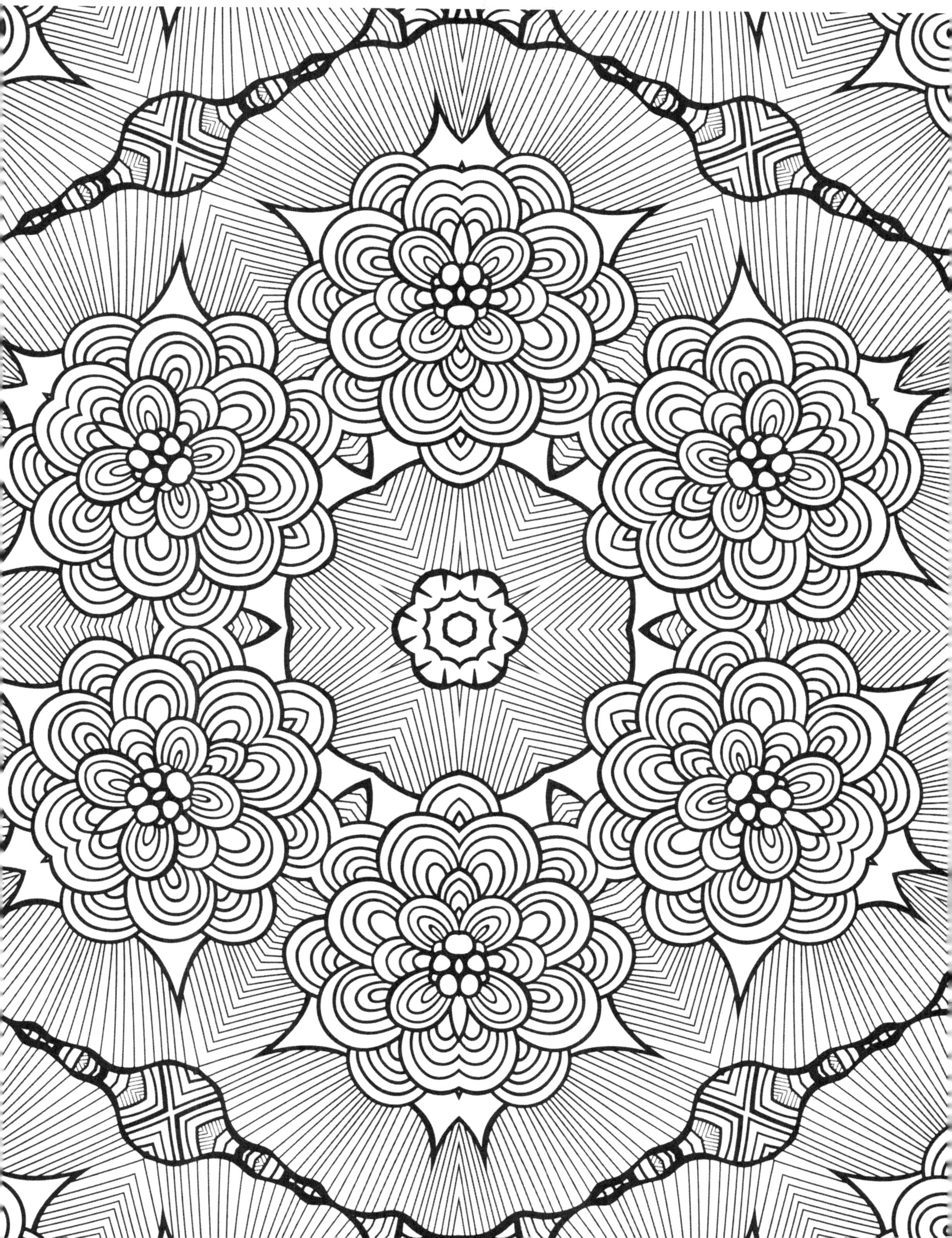

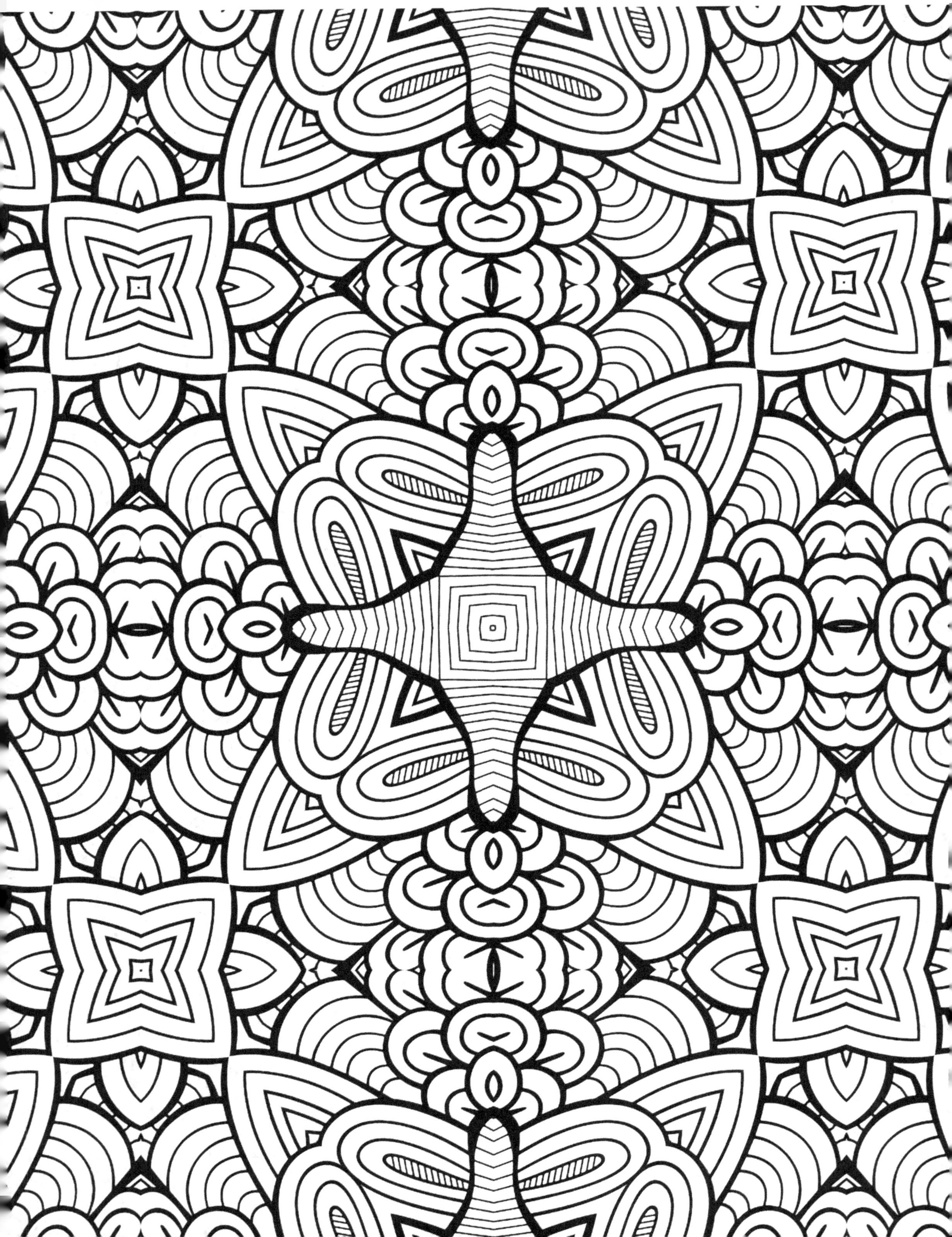

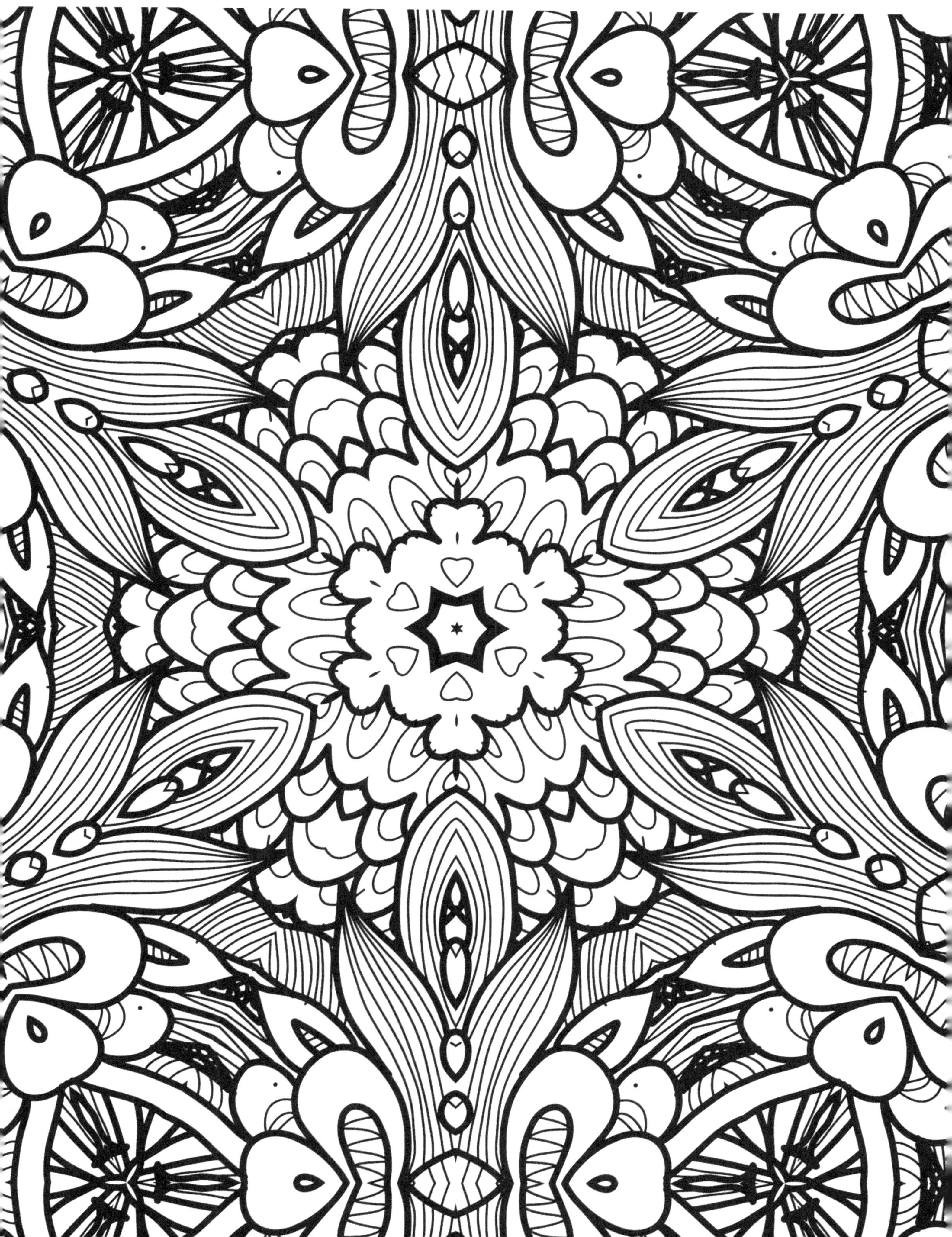

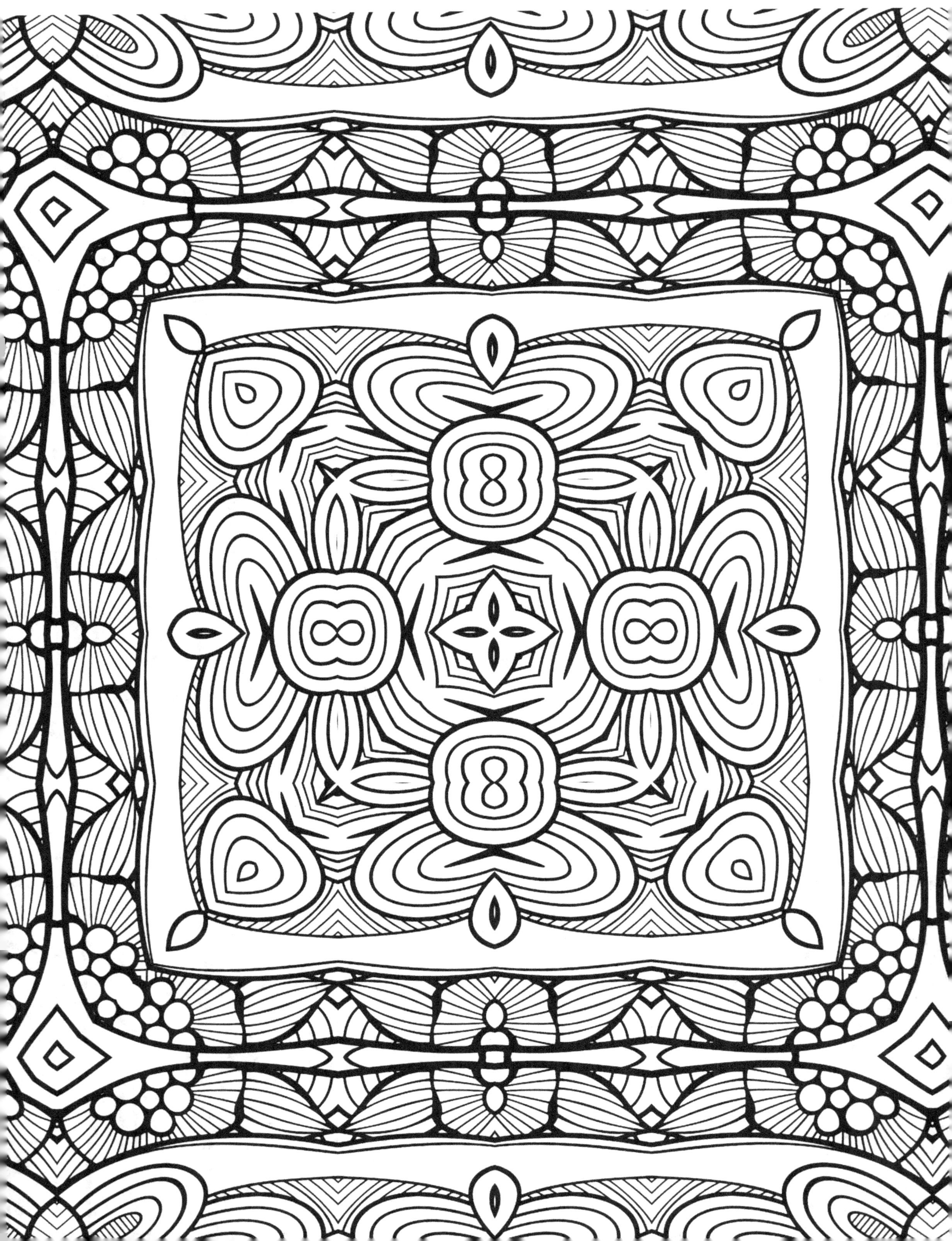

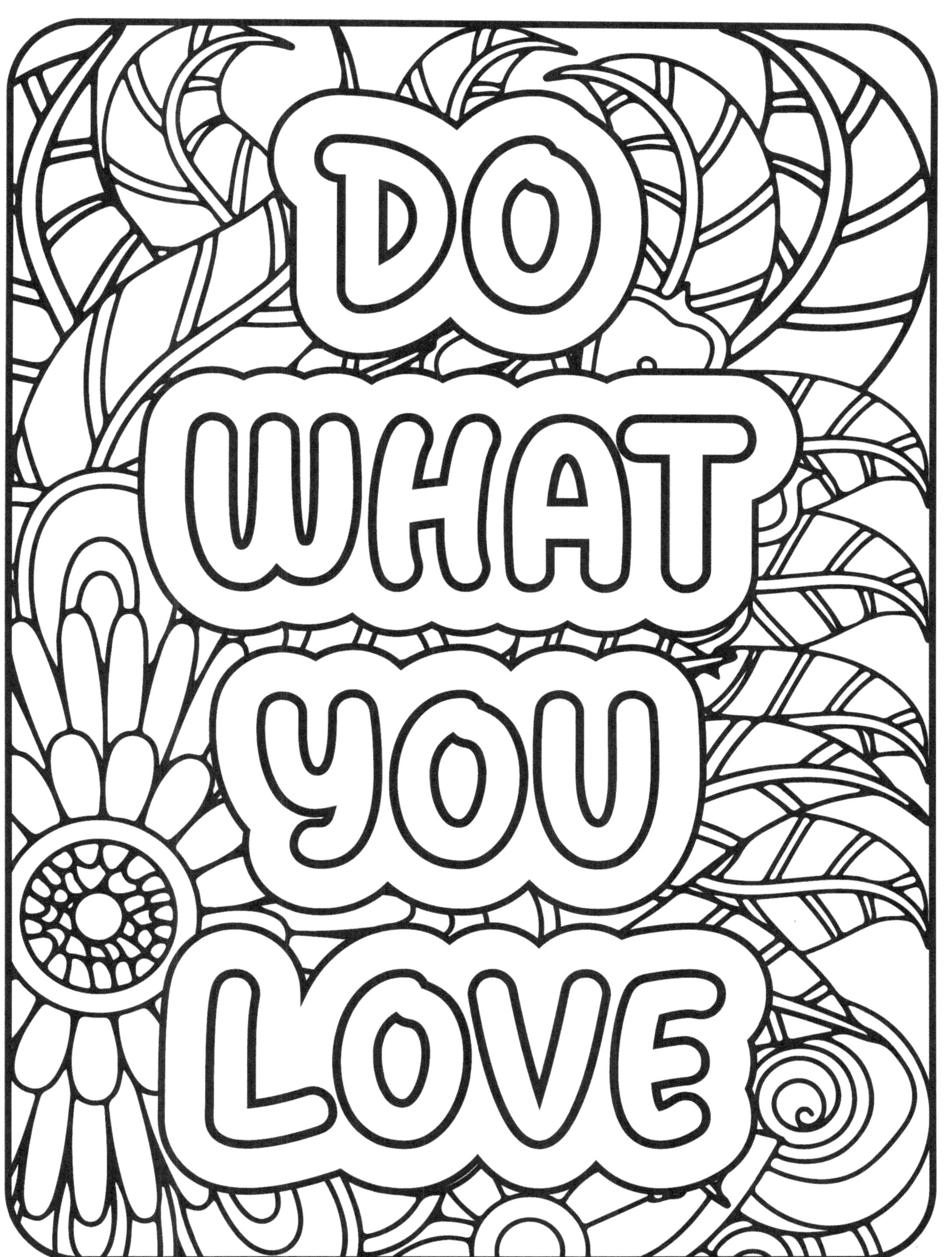

DO
WHAT
YOU
LOVE